TRANSPORTATION AFTER DEREGULATION

RESEARCH IN TRANSPORTATION ECONOMICS

Series Editor: B. Starr McMullen

Recent volumes:

Volume 1–5: Research in Transportation Economics

RESEARCH IN TRANSPORTATION ECONOMICS VOLUME 6

TRANSPORTATION AFTER DEREGULATION

EDITED BY

B. STARR McMULLEN
Department of Economics, Oregon State University, USA

2001

JAI
An Imprint of Elsevier Science

Amsterdam – London – New York – Oxford – Paris – Shannon – Tokyo

ELSEVIER SCIENCE Ltd
The Boulevard, Langford Lane
Kidlington, Oxford OX5 1GB, UK

First edition 2001

Library of Congress Cataloging in Publication Data

Transportation after deregulation / edited by B. Starr McMullen.
p. cm. – (Research in transportation economics; v. 6)
ISBN 0-7623-0780-3
1. Transportation–Deregulation. I. B. Starr McMullen, II. Series.

HE193.T6486 2001
388'.049–dc21 2001046018

British Library Cataloguing in Publication Data
A catalogue record from the British Library has been applied for.

ISBN: 0-7623-0780-3
ISSN: 0739-8859 (Series)

Transferred to digital printing 2005
Printed and bound by Antony Rowe Ltd, Eastbourne

CONTENTS

LIST OF CONTRIBUTORS

Taggert J. Brooks	Department of Economics, University of Wisconsin-Eau Claire, USA
C. Gregory Bereskin	Associate Professor, St. Ambrose University, USA
Atreya Chakraborty	Charles River Associates, Boston, USA
Mark Kazarosian	Department of Economics, Stonehill College, USA
Kristen A. Monaco	Associate Professor of Economics, California State University-Long Beach, USA
Frank W. Rusco	Senior Economist, U.S. General Accounting Office, Washington D.C., USA
W. David Walls	Associate Professor, Department of Economics, University of Calgary, Canada
Wesley W. Wilson	Department of Economics, University of Oregon, USA
William W. Wilson	Department of Agricultural Economics, North Dakota State University, USA
Lawrence Wong	Senior Research Analyst, Oregon Department of Transportation, USA

PREFACE

INTRODUCTION

The general theme for this volume is deregulation and regulatory reform in transportation industries. It is purposely broad for several reasons. First, different types of regulatory changes have been implemented in different industries. Some industries such as airlines and trucking, have been virtually deregulated and their respective regulatory agencies (the Civil Aeronautics Board (CAB) and the Interstate Commerce Commission (ICC)) have been entirely phased out of existence. Despite the demise of the ICC as the rail regulatory authority, the U.S. railroad industry operates subject to considerable economic regulation by the Surface Transportation Board (STB) which is part of the U.S. Department of Transportation (U.S.D.O.T.). Additionally, there are some transport sectors, especially in the transit area, where regulated carriers co-exist with unregulated carriers. Thus, when we speak of deregulation or regulatory reform, we can be looking at any of the above situations or possible movements from one type of regulatory scenario to another.

Second, in the more competitive market environment fostered by regulatory changes, policymakers have to deal with issues that were not expected in the deregulated setting. For instance, in both airlines and motor carriage, industries long considered to exhibit constant returns to scale, deregulators did not anticipate increases in industry concentration. However, that is precisely what has happened, especially in large hub airport markets and in less-than-truckload (LTL) motor carriage. This raises concerns regarding whether the concentration is growing due to some sorts of economies not measured by economies of scale or a form of anti-competitive behavior.

There has also been an increase in concentration in the railroad industry where in 1978 there were 37 Class I railroads in the U.S. but only 7 remained as of 2001. Some increase in concentration had been expected considering that the industry first came under economic regulation because of its natural monopoly cost structure.

Unlike railroads, most studies indicate constant returns to scale (Corsi, Grimm & Jarrell, 1987; McMullen & Lee, 1992), in both the pre- and post-regulated motor carrier industry. There is considerable evidence that there are still significant unexploited economies from increases in traffic on existing route structures, or route density. In particular, firms can reduce per unit costs by increasing average loads. If firms with larger network structures are able to more efficiently direct traffic so as to increase average loads, then observed increases in firm size may be due to these networking economies. The question for policymakers then is whether the lower costs from these networking economies are passed along to shippers in terms of lower rates or whether the firms are enjoying monopoly profit.

Preliminary studies of the deregulated motor carrier industry (Nebesky, McMullen & Lee, 1995; and Tang, 1999) find no evidence that monopoly power is being exerted to earn excess economic profit. The situation differs somewhat in the airline industry where there remains some controversy regarding the relationship between market dominance and average fares in large airport markets. Morrison and Winston (2000) argue that even if there is some monopoly power being exerted, it must be shown that the costs of this non-competitive result outweigh the benefits that have resulted from deregulation, before any serious attempt to re-regulate is considered.

While economic profits fell in both airlines and trucking following deregulation, rail profits increased. However, it must be kept in mind that regulatory reform in the railroad industry was implemented largely to help unprofitable firms increase earnings enough to remain in business – a situation much different than the case in the highly profitable regulated truck and airline industries. To date there has been no evidence of overall monopoly profits being earned by railroads. In markets where there are captive shippers (such as coal markets) there are still regulatory restrictions on pricing to prevent the possible abuse of monopoly power.

Another way in which regulatory reform or deregulation continues to impact transportation has been in the area of technology. ICC regulators often implemented policies which discouraged the adoption of new, cost-saving technologies, an example being the ICC's refusal to let railroads pass along the lower cost of Big John Hopper cars to shippers in the form of lower rail rates (Keeler, 1983). Not only did regulators prevent adoption of available cost saving technologies, their actions undoubtedly discouraged technological innovation related to transportation. Accordingly, one would expect to see technological advances in the less regulated industry proceeding at a more rapid pace, leading to increases in productivity. It is inevitable that these new technologies will change the face of transportation as it was known in the twentieth century, especially in regard to business practices and strategies.

Safety, although still regulated, is still a topic of debate in the less regulated transportation industries. In Congressional hearings preceding deregulation, it was often argued that making firms compete would result in lower profit, putting them under pressure to reduce costs in any way possible. If firms chose to reduce maintenance and other expenditures related to safety, it was argued that the result would be higher accident rates and more fatalities. On the other hand, a firm with a higher incidence of accidents may be perceived by shippers as being less reliable, thus giving carriers incentive to continue to maintain safety standards so as to keep customers. There has been no ultimate resolution of this issues, but policymakers remain concerned about any changes in safety that may have been caused by deregulation. Indeed, a high priority at the U.S.D.O.T. is to reduce the number of accidents involving heavy trucks.

The six papers included in volume 6 of *Research in Transportation Economics* all relate to the general theme of transportation deregulation/regulatory reform. Topics covered in this volume fall into one or more of the following categories: (1) the timing and impacts of deregulation, (2) new technologies, technological change, and productivity growth, (3) railroad mergers, and (4) safety. The contributions of the papers included here will be discussed next.

THE TIMING OF DEREGULATORY IMPACTS

To more accurately assess the impact of deregulation, it is necessary to determine when the major impacts of deregulation were realized so that subsequent change can be properly attributed to other factors such as advances in technology and business logistics. Three of the papers in this volume explicitly address the question of the timing of the impacts of deregulation or, as the case of railroads, regulatory reform. The first paper, by Wilson and Wilson, develops an econometric model to examine shipping rates over time for a select group of grains. Their model includes demand, cost, and pricing relationships based on the NEIO (New Empirical Industrial Organization) literature, and a specification for regulatory regime that includes both a dummy intercept and a time trend for regulatory reform (rather than simply a pre-post 1980 dummy for regulatory reform). The deregulatory time trend is specified as linear prior to 1981 when railroads had many fewer rate options and rates did not fluctuate greatly, and non-linear for the period following the Staggers Act of 1980. They use this time trend specification to show the cumulative impact of regulation reform and technological change on the rail rates through 1995 using a 1972–1995 data set. Findings show real rail rate reductions ranging from 40–71% across commodities by 1995 with the initial effects being between 2 and 19%. Although there is no direct test of market power in this study, such large rate reductions are not consistent with the exercise of market power in most circumstances. The rate reductions were made possible by a large and immediate one-shot increase in productivity (as proxied by the time trend) with results dissipating over time. They attribute the productivity gains to important provisions of the Staggers Rail Act of 1980 (SRA) which encouraged more efficient shipping practices such as allowing firms to abandon unprofitable lines and making it easier and quicker for rail firms to merge.

Note that some post-regulatory productivity advances are directly related to the post-regulatory ability to enter and leave new routes and develop a network system while others may be due to new and improved capital technologies. Although the change in regulatory regimes may have had an indirect impact on the innovation and adoption of new technologies as discussed above, the direct impact on the industry was from the the SRA's relaxation in regulations which made possible the changes in the way firms do business in the deregulated environment.

The paper by Wong takes a first step towards sorting out the independent impact of deregulation from the those changes caused by the interaction of deregulation with technology change. He uses a translog cost function with a time trend incorporated as a third order truncated Taylor series expansion, to examine the impact of deregulation and technological change in the U.S. motor carrier industry following the Motor Carrier Act of 1980 (MCA). Wong's model allows for these separate impacts (the independent impact of deregulation and the interaction between deregulation and technological change) using dummy variables and interaction terms.

This issue is particularly relevant in the motor carrier industry where deregulation led to many firms adopting marketing strategies that involve more costly service than was provided prior to deregulation. In particular, some firms have increased less-than-truckload (LTL) services which require extensive terminals and involve additional networking and coordination costs. The economy wide development of information technology has allowed firms in the deregulated setting to choose marketing strategies which focus on speed of delivery rather than just the provision of service at the lowest possible freight rate. These changes may be responsible for the seemingly contradictory results from previous cost studies which show that the industry has not experienced the expected productivity growth following deregulation (see Tang, 1999; McMullen & Lee, 1999; McMullen & Okuyama, 2000).

Wong's technique allows him to separate the impact of deregulation from the impact of deregulation on technological change, defined here to include changing business practices and marketing strategies initiated by deregulation. He finds that the direct impact of deregulation on the LTL motor carrier industry was to reduce costs by about 16.9% as of 1987, a result consistent with expectations. However, he also finds large increases in costs resulting from the interaction between deregulation and technological change. This can be explained by the expansion of LTL network systems which increased both cost and quality of service (as described above). The result that deregulation has increased the cost share of capital and reduced the cost share of fuel, is consistent with the observed increase in LTL terminals and network systems.

While most studies of the impact of deregulation arbitrarily select a point in time when the effect of deregulation is thought to have been felt and insert a discrete dummy variable into their statistical models, Monaco and Brooks use motor carrier wage data itself to determine when the structural changes impacted trucking labor. In an approach not often seen in transportation studies, they implement time series techniques and monthly data from 1972 to 1996 to examine the wage premium of truck wages over those in general manufacturing. They examine this premium rather than trucking wages alone, to sort out the independent effects of deregulation from those of the general economic recession during a period of time. Their results find a predictable relationship between average hourly wages in trucking and in manufacturing between 1972 and 1996 except for two structural break points, one in May 1980 and the other in June 1984. Thus they argue that the major impact from deregulation on wages was probably felt between 1980 and 1984. Using the relationship between manufacturing and trucking wages, they estimate that the initial effect of deregulation was to decrease average hourly trucking wages by 6.99%, resulting in a cumulative decrease of 12.43% by 1996. In addition to pinpointing the timing of the impact of deregulation on trucking wages, the decrease in wages attributable to deregulation is somewhat smaller than previous estimates which did not control for general macroeconomic events and did not utilize time series techniques.

TECHNOLOGY

Although wage effects from motor carrier deregulation were felt by 1984, other factors set lose by deregulation continue to impact productivity over time. In particular, new technologies have been developed and implemented since there are no longer regulatory policies that discourage firms from adopting new, cost saving technologies. New technologies make it possible for firms to operate differently than they did in the past. As noted above, LTL trucking firms have tended to adopt different types of marketing strategies following deregulation. In particular, on-time performance, considered an important determinant of service quality to shippers, has been adopted by many carriers rather than a "low freight rate" strategy.

Conducting efficient, on-time service requires very quick and accurate information being processed between the shipper, the trucking firm, and the on-road drivers. The ability to track, coordinate, and dispatch a fleet of trucks efficiently is made easier by the adoption of sophisticated information systems such as satellite communications, on-board computers, cell phones, and other communications and planning technologies.

Although the paper by Wong examines productivity change, his methodology cannot attribute the gain to any one particular source. This is due, in part, to the fact that he did not have data available on new technologies that could have allowed him to measure their impact on productivity. Similarly, Wong could only speculate that the changing marketing strategies used by LTL trucking firms were responsible for cost increases due to the interaction between technology and deregulation dummies in his model.

Although they do not directly analyze trucking costs, Chakrabortny and Kazarosian have used previously unavailable data to examine the relationship between the marketing strategy and the information technology used by trucking firms. They argue that high technology information gathering systems are more likely to be used by firms concerned with timely delivery since these systems allow them to track, coordinate, and dispatch their fleets in the most effective manner possible. Another firm may produce the same number of tonmiles (output), but provide that service with considerable delay if it is not concerned with time in transit, but providing the lowest possible fare – thus not requiring the same information technology. This may be part of the reason for inconclusive results regarding the impact of technology on productivity when these two sorts of firms are aggregated without controlling for marketing strategy.

The contribution from Chakrabortny and Karazorian utilizes a data set which includes information on both marketing strategy and information technology for 755 U.S. trucking firms in 1998. Using both probit and ordered probit techniques, they find that increasingly sophisticated use of information technologies depends strongly on a firm's stated market objective. As expected, for those firms with on time performance strategies, a 25% increase in time sensitive hauls increases the probability of using sophisticated information technologies by 5%. For those firms with other marketing strategies, the same increase in the number of time sensitive hauls has no statistically significant impact on technology use. Although this study does not explicitly consider trucking productivity, its results suggest that earlier findings regarding motor carrier productivity may well be due to the failure to distinguish between firm's marketing strategies. This is a possible topic for future research.

MERGERS IN THE U.S. RAILROAD INDUSTRY

There has been a considerable increase in concentration in U.S. railroad markets following passage of the SRA. The consolidations that have taken place were fostered by the Act's simplification of merger applications and proceedings. The result is that there are only two major western and two major eastern railroads, a fact leading to concerns regarding further mergers. Bereskin's paper develops a translog rail cost model using data from 1983–1999 to examine the impact on costs that would occur if there were to be a merger between one of the eastern and one of the western railroads, resulting in a single transcontinental railroad. Given the four carriers, there are four different cross-country rail mergers which he considers assuming that 1999 rail traffic volumes were to remain constant in the merger scenario. The results of his simulation show economies of scale resulting from all of the proposed mergers, resulting in lower per unit costs for the merged firms.

Bereskin's finding of unexploited economies of scale is consistent with traditional thought on the market structure of the railroad industry and the original rationale for regulation of this transportation industry to prevent monopoly pricing. However, railroads today operate in an environment that faces intermodal as well as intramodal competition, unlike the situation at the turn of the last century. Several studies (MacDonald, 1989; McMullen, 1991) show that the presence of intermodal competition (either from truck or water modes) curbs the pricing of railroad firms for bulk agricultural products. In most cases, intermodal competition should be sufficient to prevent the monopoly railroads resulting from a transcontinental merger, from exercising monopoly pricing. In cases where there is no intermodal competition, the Surface Transportation Board continues to apply guidelines related to stand alone cost pricing for coal shipments, criteria they could easily implement for other commodities as well.

As Baumol and Willig (1999) point out, in order to maintain long run financial viability in this struggling industry, stand alone cost pricing should only be used for total origin destination point trips, and not for each individual trip segment. There is still the need for further improvements in railroad finances before the continued private operation of the railroad industry in the U.S. will be certain. Thus, even with only seven railroads in current operation, it is not likely that further increases in concentration will remedy the financial problem from the revenue side since there does not appear to be evidence that the railroads are able to exploit their monopoly position to drive up prices. Thus, the only viable option for increasing industry profit and maintain a private rail industry in the U.S., may be to encourage further cost saving activities. Bereskin's results suggest that a transcontinental merger might well help achieve this goal.

Note that in the cases Bereskin considers, he assumes 1999 traffic levels. Potential benefits from mergers may well produce increased traffic for transcontinental movements since a single rail company may be able to offer more efficient, higher quality service to shippers, thus diverting traffic from other modes (truckload motor carriers in particular). Accordingly, the cost savings from such mergers might well be considerably greater than Bereskin's model suggests.

SAFETY

Finally, the question of safety in a regulated versus a non-regulated market continues to be a topic of great concern to policymakers. The final paper in this volume deals with minibus passenger transit in Hong Kong where there are essentially two bus systems operating in the city, one that is subject to considerable regulation and the other that is relatively unregulated. Rusco and Walls set up a model which suggests that the unregulated minibuses have the incentive to drive faster and thus are expected to have higher accident rates than their regulated counterparts. They test this hypothesis using data for Hong Kong and find that the less regulated buses have both higher accident rates and lower travel times than the regulated buses.

Interestingly enough, their data also shows an increase in the number of regulated buses relative to unregulated buses. This is true in a system where there is a fixed total number of buses and the number of unregulated buses are determined as a residual after the demand for regulated buses is fulfilled. This suggests that consumers recognize the poorer safety records of the unregulated buses and this has created a market where they are willing to pay more for safer, slower service and both regulated and unregulated firms co-exists in the same market. Obviously, such a scenario would not be feasible in the trucking industry, for instance, where the major costs imposed by unsafe trucks are on other users of the highway system, rather than the customer (shipper).

The major contribution of this paper is that it illustrates one clear case where both theory and empirical evidence support the conclusion that unregulated firms are less safe than regulated firms. However, this result should be interpreted with care given the obvious dissimilarities between passenger transit and intercity freight service.

CONCLUSIONS

The papers included in this volume all contain important policy implications. The first three papers document the fact that the impacts from changes in rail regulations and trucking deregulation had their main impacts on costs, wages, and rates well before the 1990s. Other factors, such as increases in technology and changing marketing strategies in trucking, and mergers in rail, are probably responsible for subsequent industry productivity changes. Indeed, several of these papers delve into the relationship between marketing strategy, technology, and productivity – which is bound to be the direction of future research in the more competitive market environment of the 21st century.

The paper on minibus competition in Hong Kong reminds us that there may still be a role for government intervention/regulation in the transportation sector when the unregulated market is unable to provide something such as an acceptable level of safety. While deregulation has been the trend at the turn of the century, some of the issues raised in this volume will be factors considered by policymakers in the future when deciding on which, if any, future regulations are necessary in the transportation industries.

REFERENCES

Baumol, R. J., & Willig, R.D (1999). Competitive Rail Regulation Rules: Should Price Ceilings Constrain Final Products or Inputs? *Journal of Transport Economics and Policy*, *33*, 43–54.

Grimm, C. M., Corsi, T. M., & Jarrell, J. L. (1989). U.S. Motor Carrier Cost Structure Under Deregulation. *Logistics and Transportation Review*, *25*, 231–249.

Keeler, T. E. (1983) *Railroads, Freight, and Public Policy*. Washington D.C.: The Brookings Institution.

MacDonald, J. M. (1989). Railroad Deregulation, Innovation, and Competition: Effects of the Staggers Act of Grain Transportation. *Journal of Law and Economics*, *32*, 63–95.

McMullen, B. S. (1987). The Impact of Regulatory Reform on U.S. Motor Carrier Costs. *Journal of Transportation Economics and Policy*, *21*, 307–319.

McMullen, B. S. (1991). Determinants of Wheat Transportation Rates for Pacific Northwest Shippers. *Journal of the Transportation Research Forum*, *32*, 9–16.

McMullen, B. S., & Lee, M. (1993). Assessing the Impact of Regulatory Reform on Motor Carrier Costs. *Journal of the Transportation Research Forum*, *33*, 1–9.

McMullen, B. S., & Lee, M. (1999). Cost Efficiency in the U.S. Motor Carrier Industry Before and After Deregulation: A Stochastic Frontier Approach. *Journal of transport Economics and Policy*, *33*, 303–317.

McMullen, B. S., & Okuyama, K. (2000). Productivity Changes in the U.S. Motor Carrier Industry Following Deregulation: A Malmquist Approach. *International Journal of Transport Economics*, *27*, 335–354.

Morrison, S. A., & Winston, C. (2000). The Remaining Role for Government Policy in the Deregulated Airline Industry. In: S. Peltzman & C. Winston (Eds), *Deregulation of Network Industries: What's Next?* (pp. 1–40). Washington, D.C.: AEI-Brookings institution Joint Center for Regulatory Studies.

Nebesky, W. E., McMullen, B. S., & Lee, M. (1995). Testing for Market Power in the U.S. Motor Carrier Industry. *Review of Industrial Organization*, *10*, 559–576.

Tang, A. P. (1999). *Impacts of Deregulation on the Performance of Trucking Firms*. Baltimore, MD: National Transportation Center, Morgan State University.

DEREGULATION, RATE INCENTIVES, AND EFFICIENCY IN THE RAILROAD MARKET

Wesley W. Wilson and William W. Wilson

ABSTRACT

A number of important innovations and events over the last 25 years have reshaped railroad marketing and have led to dramatically lower rates. Many of these innovations have been developed for and used extensively in agricultural markets. In this paper, we document these innovations and examine the behavior of rail rates from 1972–1995, using a nonlinear regulatory adjustment mechanism to represent the effects of partial deregulation. We focus on rate changes that have occurred under the new regulatory regime introduced by passage of the Staggers Rail Act in 1980. Our econometric analysis applies to the five leading agricultural commodities shipped by rail which account for over 90% of agricultural movements. We find that rates for all five commodities have fallen dramatically over time, but that there are differences across the commodities in magnitude. We also find that the effect of partial deregulation on rates and productivity, while large, dissipates over time.

Transportation After Deregulation, Volume 6, pages 1–24.

ISBN: 0-7623-0780-3

1. INTRODUCTION

Tremendous changes have occurred in the rail industry since partial deregulation.[1] Prior to partial deregulation, rates and networks were slow to adjust and innovation was virtually non-existent due to price regulation and rail line abandonment impediments (i.e. network regulation). The Staggers Rail Act (SRA) of 1980 gave railroads much more discretion over rates and network than before passage. With this discretion, railroads introduced a number of innovative pricing mechanisms. Associated with these pricing mechanisms were service options that dramatically improved railroad efficiency which, in turn, led to decreases in rail rates.

While rail rates are lower, shippers are concerned. Under deregulation, there have been significant alterations to the rail network both in terms of size and ownership. These alterations have been due largely to reduced regulatory impediments to mergers and rail line abandonment/sales. The effects of a smaller rail network held by fewer railroads, have fed shipper concerns about competitive access, service deficiencies, railroad performance, the level of product and geographic competition, and the continuing effects of rail mergers (*National Grain and Feed Association*, 1997, 1998). These concerns have been expressed to the *Surface Transportation Board* (STB) along with proposals for regulatory reform.

In this paper, we provide a short description of innovations introduced since partial deregulation and analyze the effects of partial deregulation on rates. We develop and estimate a model of rates that allows for rates and productivity to adjust nonlinearly to partial deregulation. Using our adjustment mechanism, the effects of partial deregulation vary over time with the largest incremental effects experienced soon after partial deregulation. Over time, the total effects of partial deregulation continue to reduce rates but at a slower rate.[2]

Many of the innovations introduced under partial deregulation were directed at bulk commodities, and in particular, at agricultural commodities. Therefore, we focus our analysis on the five leading agricultural commodities shipped by rail. We find that partial deregulation had a negative effect on rates and a positive effect on productivity. However, there are considerable differences across commodities in terms of the magnitudes of the rate and productivity effects of partial deregulation. We also find the effects of partial deregulation on rates and productivity increase in magnitude over time but do so at a dissipating rate. This finding suggests that the most efficiency enhancing innovations occurred soon after partial deregulation with progressively less dramatic innovations occurring over time. Thus, while the effects of partial deregulation and innovation are substantial, our findings suggest these effects have largely run their course. As a result, further regulatory reform may not have much of a potential to reduce rates further and may run the risk of reversing the already large effects.

2. PREVIOUS STUDIES

A number of studies have examined the effects of partial deregulation of railroads. Many of these early studies, conducted in the period immediately following partial deregulation, used optimization e.g. Fuller, Makus and Taylor (1983), Fuller and Shanmugham (1981) or simulation techniques e.g. Levin (1981). In agricultural markets, early studies e.g. Klindworth, Sorenson, Babcock and Chow (1985), Adam and Anderson (1985) used spatial commodity price spreads as a proxy for rail rates to examine changes after partial deregulation. These studies examined periods soon after partial deregulation and, as a result, may not reflect the full impact.[3]

Other more recent studies use econometric analysis of actual changes in rates for various levels of aggregation across commodities, regions and competitive environments. At an aggregate level, Boyer (1987), McFarland (1989), Barnekov and Kliet (1990), and MacDonald and Cavalluzzo (1996) examine the average rate for all commodities and all movements over time and across regulatory regime. They offer mixed conclusions, finding modest increases, no change, and substantial rate decreases in the rate level from partial deregulation. Burton (1993) and Wilson (1994) examine average rate levels for specific but aggregated commodity movements. These studies find small initial effects for different commodities with larger negative effects occurring over time. This latter finding applies to all commodities, although there are important differences in the magnitude of these effects across commodities. In virtually all of the previous research that finds negative effects of partial deregulation, the negative effects are attributed to reductions in costs. As discussed in MacDonald and Cavalluzzo (1996), Berndt, Friedlacnder, Chiang and Vellturo (1993), Vellturo, Berndt, Friedlaender, Chiang and Showalter (1992), and Wilson (1994, 1997), the primary effects of partial deregulation on costs are the result of more consolidated shipments with longer lengths of haul, the abandonment and sale of unprofitable rail lines, and the dramatic consolidation of firms.

Of most relevance to this analysis are the studies pertaining to agricultural commodities.[4] There are several studies modeling agricultural rail rates for different commodities. These include Hauser (1986), MacDonald (1986, 1989), Adam and Anderson (1985), Klindworth et al. (1985), Fuller, Bessler, MacDonald and Wohlgenant (1987), and Wilson, Wilson and Koo (1988). These studies vary in the level of aggregation, commodity, and region of analysis, but each find that partial deregulation has a negative influence on agricultural rail rates. Other studies e.g. Thompson, Hauser and Couglin (1990) and Fuller et al. (1983) found no effect or found mixed results.

Many of the previous studies use an intercept shift and/or a broken trend to model the time-related effects of partial deregulation. However, the full effects likely result from an adjustment process as lawmakers and regulators dismantle regulatory regimes and firms adjust to a new competitive environment (Winston, 1998). In most of the previous literature, the effects of partial deregulation have been introduced by a dummy variable sometimes interacted with a linear time trend and are often focused on a specific commodity. Our approach to modeling the behavior of rates over time allows for gradual initial effects that grow over time at a decreasing rate eventually reaching an asymptote which can be interpreted as the long-run effect of partial deregulation on rates and on productivity. Our treatment removes the unfortunate characteristic of a linear trend that allows the effects of partial deregulation to grow without bound. In addition to the identification of the long-term effects of partial deregulation on rates and productivity, we also conduct the analysis for the five major agricultural commodities, accounting for over 90% of agricultural movements. The model is estimated separately for each of the five commodities but use common data and specifications which allow comparisons to be made across commodities.

3. DEREGULATION AND EFFICIENCY INDUCING PRICING MECHANISMS

Beginning in the mid-1970s, regulatory rules on rail rate-making started to become much more flexible relative to historical rules. Prior to the mid-1970s, the array of rail shipping options and rate alternatives were quite limited. A major effect of partial deregulation was the increase in the number of shipping options and its associated rates available to shippers. Through these options, considerable efficiencies have accrued in the provision of rail services with the effect of decreasing costs, and ultimately, rates. In this section, we provide an overview of the major regulatory changes and new services offered, as well as other factors that have significantly affected rates.

Partial Deregulation of Rate Determination

Beginning with the Railroad Revitalization and Regulatory Reform Act of 1976, and culminating with the passage of the Staggers Rail Act of 1980, railroad regulations were substantially altered. Prior to this period, rates were based on single-car movements, were subject to regulatory oversight, and were typically determined through a rate bureau system. While rates could adjust to changing market conditions, they adjusted with substantial lags and tended to be changes that applied to broad regional and commodity classifications.

Partial deregulation introduced the concept of market dominance in the determination of rates. Under market dominance rules, railroads could change rates without regulatory impediment if the rates were not the result of market dominant forces.[5] While market dominance did little in the way of introducing new service options for shippers or significant cost efficiencies to railroads, it did introduce pricing flexibility which allowed railroads to change rates for different configurations of movements.

In addition to the introduction of market dominance rules, partial deregulation placed constraints on the role of rate bureaus in the determination of rates. Prior to partial deregulation, rate bureaus played an extensive role in rate and service levels. While railroads had the right to independent actions, rate and service changes were subject to approval by the rate bureau. Partial deregulation limited the role of rate bureaus in independent railroad pricing decisions, reducing the role of rate bureaus to establish joint rates. The reduced role of rate bureaus and the introduction of market dominance standards served to increase the role of independent rate making by railroads, and facilitated the introduction of new rate structures and service options.

The Evolution of Innovative Service and Pricing Options

The development of multiple car rates marked one of the earliest pricing innovations and was responsible for major efficiency gains. Multiple car movements require less switching, have more efficient loading techniques, and the consolidation of larger and longer haul movements. After the introduction of multiple car rates, railroads used several different approaches to effectuate multiple car movements which led to the realization of additional efficiencies. For example, in the initial periods following partial deregulation, the BN offered a 52-car unit, a 26-car single-origin, a 26-car multiple origin, and a single-car rate with substantial differences across the service offerings. The range of multiple-car options gave railroads a range of efficiency gains, while still allowing different sized shippers to realize some of the economies gained through multiple-car movements. Over time, however, rates for multiple-origin movements, which allowed branch-line shippers with smaller facilities and limited siding to gain part of the benefits of multiple car rates, were discontinued and replaced with rates associated with other types of service options.

Coinciding with the development of multiple car rates was the formation of contracts between primarily large shippers and railroads. Generally, contract rates were considerably less than single-car rates, provided for multiple car movements and guaranteed volumes of shipment. At one point, movements under contract accounted for over 60% of agricultural movements. In 1986, confidentiality of contracts was restricted by Public Law 99-509, and the use of contracts fell dramatically.[6]

More recently, *Origin-Destination Efficiency* (ODE) programs were introduced in 1993 "to promote efficient car utilization, customer logistics, and quality accounting." The programs usually required shipment in larger units (e.g. 108 cars consisting of two 54-car units), and for the freight to be loaded at one or two stations, termination at a single destination elevator, and loading and unloading to be done within 16 hours of placement. These shipments normally required some guarantee of freight and a discount typically applies to the total movement. As with early forms of multiple car movements, railroads refined and expanded the use of ODE types of movements, leading to added efficiencies. For example, 1997, ODE type train shipments were introduced from the upper Midwest, though similar programs existed in contract form in other parts of the country and on other railroads. The various multi-car programs were developed in incremental steps in the process of improving rail efficiency. One important underlying factor is that the velocity of grain cars is far greater than for other types of movements. For example, the BNSF recently cited the average velocity (i.e. days per trip) of coal trains at 5.3 days compared with wheat trains at 19 days.[7] As such, a primary motivation for introducing such programs was to increase the productivity of the railroads. As noted by Collier, ". . . is part of our [the UP] ongoing strategy to reward the productivity of individual facilities through our rate structures."[8] Other major railroads have since implemented similar programs, though, in many cases, the terms remain under contract. The use of these programs is currently limited to selective corridors, perhaps, because the commercial viability of these mechanisms depends critically on railroad and receiver logistics.

Per-car rates are a recent innovation in the marketing of railroad services and, again, represent a source of efficiency gains. Prior to the late 1980s, virtually all rail grain rates in the upper Midwest were on a per-unit-of-volume basis (e.g. per bushel or cwt.). Since rates were on this basis, the extent of car loadings was not affected by the rate structure often resulting in less-than-fully-loaded cars. Per-car rates encourage handlers to fully load cars to capacity, resulting in loading, accounting, and billing efficiency gains. Further, since 1990, some railroads adopted larger covered hopper cars, adding to efficiency gains. For example, C6X cars have a 286,000 pound gross weight limit, allowing shippers to load approximately 11 more tons than in regular C6 covered hopper cars. Since the use and management of these cars differ, they are subject to different tariff provisions and rates.

Market Based Car Allocation Mechanisms

In 1987, due to chronic car shortages, along with the realization that different shippers have different service needs, the railroad industry began to introduce market-based car allocation mechanisms. These pricing mechanisms allow shippers to bid for these services, and those with the highest value would receive priorities in service. As with the other innovations, these programs have changed marginally over time and continue to have important implications for the grain handling and shipping industries, as well as for rail productivity.[9]

These mechanisms can be interpreted as a form of differentiated service. Under the Staggers Rail Act (SRA) "Rail carriers shall be permitted to establish tariffs containing premium charges for special services of specific levels of services not provided in any tariff otherwise applicable to the movement." (Section 10734 of Title 49, United States Code). Currently, these programs have evolved into a system of mechanisms including shorter-term guarantees, longer-term guarantees of service, and more refined procedures for allocation of general car orders. Virtually all of the major Class I railroads that provide for the transportation of agricultural programs have now developed and adopted such market based car allocation mechanisms, which facilitate the continued evolution of enhanced rail productivity through more accurate forward capacity planning and placements.

In summary, since partial deregulation, railroads have made concerted efforts to tie rates more closely to demand and to cost and competitive conditions. Partial deregulation has given railroads the opportunity to develop new rate structures that allow efficiencies to be realized. These new innovative rate structures have taken the form of multiple car rates, contract rates, premium service rates, and per-car rates. Many of these have been adopted since 1980, and were designed for agricultural movements. The result of these innovations are largely responsible for the efficiency gains and rate reductions in the rail industry.

4. ANALYSIS OF RATE LEVELS AND CHANGES

Theoretically, rates are taken as a function of four basic elements. These include demand, costs, pricing and regulatory regime.[10] In a Bresnahan (1989) "*New Empirical Industrial Organization*" framework, a model of rail rates is a function of variables representing demand, cost, and regulatory regime and is given by:[11]

$$r = MC(Q, X^C, R, \gamma) - \frac{\partial r}{\partial Q}(Q, X^D, \beta)Q\theta(R), \qquad (1)$$

where r is the rate, Q is output, X^C is a vector of cost shifters, R reflects the regulatory regime, γ is a set of cost parameters, $\partial r/\partial Q$ is the slope of the inverse demand curve, X^D is a vector of demand shifters, β is a set of demand parameters, and θ is an index of the departure of prices from marginal costs.

As in previous research (e.g. Wilson, 1994), the effects of partial deregulation can then be written as:

$$\frac{r_{it}^{PD} - r_{it}^{R}}{r_{it}^{R}} = \frac{MC_{it}^{PD}/(1 + \theta_{it}^{PD}/\eta_{it})}{MC_{it}^{R}/(1 + \theta_{it}^{R}/\eta_{it})}, \qquad (2)$$

where PD and R are subscripts for partially deregulated and regulated regimes, η is the elasticity of demand, and the effects of partial deregulation on rates are captured in the marginal cost functions and the markup parameters.

Econometrically, we base our empirical work on Eq. (1) and specify it as:[12]

$$r_{it} = r(Q_t, Q_{it}, P_{it}, X_{it}^D, X_{it}^C, t, R_t) + \varepsilon_{it}, \qquad (3)$$

where:
- r_{it} is the rate per tonmile of the ith commodity in year t;
- Q_t is the total tonmiles shipped systemwide in year t;
- Q_{it} is the total tonmiles shipped of commodity i in year t;
- P_{it} is the end-use value of commodity i in year t (e.g. the value of a bushel of wheat);
- X_{it}^D is a set of demand shifters (discussed below);
- X_{it}^C is a set of cost shifters controls (discussed below);
- t is a time index; and
- R represents the regulatory regime.

Our dependent variable is the aggregate rate per tonmile at the STCC (*Standard Commodity Transportation Code*) five digit level for agricultural commodities.[13] The 11 variables we use follow the literature with a few differences. We examine the use of two output measures, systemwide tonmiles and commodity tonmiles. The former allows for systemwide cost externalities, while the latter captures the effects of density economies. To the extent systemwide cost externalities and density economies are present and positive, the associated coefficients should be negative. We also include the end-use value of the commodity shipped. Inclusion of this variable emanates from the demand side of the model and should have a positive influence on rates. Other control variables emanate from cost considerations. These include average length of haul, average load, miles of road, as well as the variables that capture the effects of innovation and changes in regulatory regime. Both average length of haul and average load are expected to have a negative effect on costs and, therefore, on rates due to the presence of quasi-fixed factors. That is, as length of haul or loads increase, the quasi-fixed costs of shipping are spread over greater distances or tons.[14] Miles of road is a measure of network size. In most cost studies, miles of road has an increasing effect on costs and should then have an increasing effect on rates.

The time behavior of rates is a central focus of the study. It is widely regarded that rate changes associated with time were minor or non-existent prior to partial deregulation. As noted by Winston (1998) and discussed above, the effects of time on rates after partial deregulation are expected to smooth in over time. While we examine other treatments of regulatory regime shifts and time related effects, our preferred treatment is an intercept shift and interaction with the trend for partial deregulation. We use a linear time trend prior to 1981 and a non-linear trend after 1980. The nonlinear trend is given by:

$$trend = a_t\, t + a_{STAGT}\,(t\,/\,(1 + t))STAG,$$

which allows the effects of partial deregulation to be given by:

$$\frac{r^{PD} - r^{R}}{r^{R}} = (\exp(\alpha_{STAG} + (\alpha_{STAGT}\,(t\,/\,(1 + t))) - 1) * 100$$

With this treatment, we note that as time since partial deregulation increases, the productivity effects are greatest during the early periods. As time since partial deregulation increases without bound the effects converge to $(\alpha_{STAG} + \alpha_{STAGT} - 1) * 100$, the fully adjusted effect.

We note that the effects of partial deregulation are captured in the time trend and in the variables. Many of the unobserved and the observed variables are highly correlated with time. Specifically, there are tremendous efficiencies manifested in larger firm sizes in terms of output and network size but a reduced system network, higher densities, longer lengths of haul, a different traffic mix (e.g. more bulk movements), faster car turnaround, larger shipment sizes, etc. Miles of road (network size) has fallen steadily over the time period (and the correlation with the time trend in all cases is in excess of 0.99), carmiles per hour has fallen steadily over the time period, and railroads now ship a higher proportion of bulk commodities. Identification of each source of cost savings is quite difficult, given high correlations with the time trend. As a result, the variables we include in our final specification are reduced from the list above. The excluded variables, however, still represent potentially large efficiency gains, and, in fact, partially underlie our findings on the trends. In Section 6, we present two sets of results. We base most of our discussion on a specification reduced from that presented above, but also present the results for the relatively more general model above in an appendix. The former is a reflection of the collinearity in the data as well as a series of specification considerations.

We use a double-log specification in all continuous variables in estimating Eq. (3). Estimation rests on several issues. First, various right-hand test variables may be endogenous. Using Hausman (1978) tests and a comparison of OLS and instrumental estimates allow an assessment of whether treatment of these potentially endogenous variables as exogenous introduces *significant* bias. Total production of the commodity is the instrument for the tonmiles of the product transported. Various industrial production indices i.e. coal, transportation equipment, and chemicals (which along with agricultural products, represent the four leading products transported by railroads), serve as instruments for total tonmiles, average length of haul, and average load.

A second issue relates to the treatment of error terms. Specifically, the data (described below) pertain to five different commodities from 1972–1995. We examine and make appropriate corrections as necessary for serial correlation in the individual errors for each of the five commodities (using Durbin-Watson and Durbin-H statistics as appropriate).

5. DATA

Our principal source of data is the public use waybill data set. We do not use individual records. Rather, we use the expanded records which reflect the population. Most of the sampling difficulties and changes in sampling are, therefore, largely removed.[15] For the 1972–1984 period, these data were taken from the *U.S. Department of Transportation, Federal Railway Administration, 1972–1984, Carload Waybill Statistics TD-1 Report.* A variable of particular interest is the average rate per tonmile for all movements of each commodity (these are Standard Transportation Commodity Code Level 5 rates). From 1985 through 1995, the rates were generated from the Public Use Waybill data. In total, there are 120 observations, representing five commodities over a twenty-four year period.

The waybill data include rail rates, quantities, and movements characteristics. Data were also taken from *Railroad Facts* (Association of American Railroads, *Railroad Facts*, Various Years) including total tonmiles, miles of track and road, and net tonmiles per hour. Data on grain production (in 1000 tons) and prices (in $/ton) were taken from USDA *Agricultural Statistics*. Finally, data were taken from the Department of Commerce on producer price index [PPIFG = Producer price index for finished goods (base = 1982)] and the GNP price deflator [GNPPD = GNP price deflator (base = 1992)].

A summary of the data reveals a number of observations. First, there has been an increase in tonmiles shipped by rail for each commodity. Second, both average length of haul and load per car have increased. Third, the number of miles operated (MOR) have decreased tremendously since partial deregulation. These three factors point to cost efficiencies through the variables. Finally, and key to the findings on partial deregulation, are the changes in rates. In the period following 1980, real rates for all commodities decreased, by an average of 52% (ranging from 40–71%), indicating the magnitude of changes under partial deregulation.

6. RESULTS

Our purpose in the empirical estimation is to identify the dynamic behavior of rates across regulatory regimes. The dependent variable in all cases is the deflated rate of the commodity per tonmile.[16] The effects of time and partial deregulation are particularly important in this analysis. With respect to the treatment of trends, we use a linear trend prior to partial deregulation and a nonlinear trend after partial deregulation. We report the results obtained from a linear trend through the passage of Staggers (trend = 1 for 1972, trend = 2 for 1973, etc.) and a nonlinear trend beginning with the passage of Staggers. Until the passage of Staggers, the trend is given by $\alpha_t t$. If rate changes are impacted by improved technological change, the coefficient should be negative. However, under the regulatory environment, induced technological change are commonly thought to be quite small. Accordingly, the coefficient should not be statistically different from zero.

Post-Staggers effects on productivity are based on the conjecture and common wisdom that the initial effects are quite small and grow with time at a decreasing rate (Winston, 1998). Previous research commonly treats the adjustments to a switch in regulatory regime through the use of a dummy variable which has sometimes been interacted with a linear trend. Results of such specifications have the property of instantaneous adjustment, in the case of the dummy variable model, and of adjustments that become implausible over time, in the case of the model with dummy and trend interactions.

We also examined several different trends including linear, quadratic, and cubic adjustments. Pre-Staggers linear trend specifications yield no statistically significant effects of time on rates. The post-Staggers linear trend specifications yielded negative effects that were statistically significant for barley and sorghum. For corn, the negative effects were small in magnitude, but not statistically significant, while for wheat and soybeans, the effects of Staggers on the trend was positive, but not statistically significant. Quadratic trends fit the data well. However, rapid initial effects of partial deregulation with respect to time cause the effects of Staggers to reverse the trend. In the cases in which the effect of Staggers reversed the trend, the switching point occurred in the late 1980s. To further examine this property, we considered both cubic trend models and various switching point models.[17] These considerations were of little success, with considerable insignificance in the trend terms (only in one case did the specification yield significant results). In addition, these effects were not materially different from the preferred specification. Due to these considerations, we use the non-linear trend discussed earlier i.e. $\text{trend} = \alpha_t\, t + \alpha_{STAGT}[t/(1 + t)]STAG$. This specification allows for the effects of Staggers to follow a nonlinear pattern, with the largest effect (with respect to time) in the initial periods following partial deregulation. Further, the rate of time change due to this trend also results in Staggers having large initial effects that dissipate with time. The long-term effect is an asymptote given by $\alpha_t + \alpha_{STAGT}$.

We base the remainder of the paper on the specification as reported in Table 1 (versus the fully specified model in Table A1). Our specification yields a more general model than in related studies. We estimate the general model and then examine the robustness of our results to alternative specifications. Our inspection of the data indicates that there are significant correlations between average load, system tonmiles and miles of load[18] with the time and trend. However, the results are not qualitatively affected by their exclusion. Quantitatively, there is some effect on the results discussed below, owing largely to the correlation between these variables and the STAG and trend variables. These variables are generally not statistically significant for all specifications. Because of the limited degrees of freedom and the high degree of multicollinearity among these variables with the STAG and trend effects, we exclude them from the model. We do note, however, that because these variables are correlated with the coefficients of interest, their effects are represented in the model, and, in part, explain the results below.[19]

In both the full specification, and those reported in Table 1, serial correlation corrections were necessary only for wheat. Consequently, the OLS results are reported with the exception of wheat, which was estimated using maximum likelihood iterative techniques. The fit in all specifications is extremely high with adjusted R-squares in excess of 0.96. Further, the statistically significant coefficients are generally consistent with prior expectations.

The results discussed below are from Table 1. Commodity tonmiles has a negative effect on rates in all specifications. However, these estimates are statistically significant only for wheat and for soybeans. In these two cases, a 1% increase in tonmiles reduces rates by 0.25%. Because of the potential for

Table 1. Reduced Specification Regression Results by Commodity.

	Commodity				
	Barley	Corn	Sorghum	Wheat	Soybeans
Constant	−2.08*	−3.83*	−2.51	0.41	−0.68
	(1.70)	(2.48)	(1.48)	(0.19)	(0.36)
Commodity	−0.11	−0.06	−0.04	−0.25*	−0.25*
Ton Miles	(1.31)	(0.49)	(0.50)	(1 98)	(2.07)
Commodity	0.11*	0.24*	0.17*	0.06	0.24*
Price	(2.08)	(4.03)	(1.83)	(0.70)	(2.11)
Avg. Length of	−0.61*	−0.66*	−0.86*	−0.43*	−0.54*
Haul	(4.00)	(2.35)	(4.84)	(2.01)	(2.40)
SRA	10.96*	9.18 *	13.88 *	10.39*	6.01*
	(5.95)	(3.07)	(4.83)	(1.78)	(1.88)
Pre-Staggers	0.01	−0.02	0.01	0.01	0.02
Trend	(0.99)	(1.56)	(0.87)	(0.16)	(1.16)
Post-Staggers	−12.17*	−10.21 *	−15.29*	−11.59*	−6.8*
Trend	(6.00)	(3.12)	(4.83)	(1.80)	(1.95)
Adj. R^2	0.99	0.98	0.96	0.98	0.98
DW	1.72	1.94	1.68	1.77	1.46

Values in ( ) are the t-statistic and * indicates significance at the 10% level.

commodity tonmiles to introduce bias into estimation by OLS, we also estimated the model by excluding commodity tonmiles from the specification. The results of interest – the adjustment of rates over time – are not affected qualitatively and are nearly identical numerically.

Inclusion of commodity price results from demand-side considerations and should positively affect rates. It has a positive effect in all specifications and is statistically significant for all commodities except for wheat. For the statistically significant effects, a 1% increase in the commodity price increases the rate per tonmile by 0.11% for barley, 0.24% for corn, 0.17% for sorghum, and 0.24% for soybeans. The significance of this variable is important in that it has a clear interpretation of a demand-side variable, illustrating that rates change with changes in demand and are not fueled entirely by cost changes.

Average length of haul has a universally negative and statistically significant effect on rates. A 1% increase in ALH reduces rates by 0.61% for barley, 0.66% for corn, 0.86% for sorghum, 0.43% for wheat, and 0.54% for soybeans. Virtually all empirical specifications in previous research include average length of haul based on cost considerations. Traffic movements have quasi-fixed factors and longer lengths of haul allow these factors to be spread out over greater distances. The magnitudes of each coefficient suggests that these changes are an important source of rate reductions under Staggers. In particular, from 1981 to 1995, ALH increased about 62% for barley, 15% for corn, 67% for sorghum, 73% for wheat, and 65% for soybeans. The effect of these changes translate into a 38% reduction in barley rates, a 10% reduction in corn rates, a 58% reduction in sorghum rates, a 31% reduction in wheat rates, and a 35% reduction in soybean rates.

The remaining results pertain to the dynamic effects of rate changes and regulatory regime effects. The results are consistent across specifications. Prior to partial deregulation, there is no evidence of a trend. In all cases, the coefficient on the linear trend is small in magnitude and statistically insignificant in all specifications, providing strong evidence against significant technological progress in the 1970s.[20] The interaction of Staggers with the nonlinear trend is, in contrast, statistically significant in all specifications (at the 10% level), suggesting that the annual percent change from partial deregulation is negative and statistically significant.

To examine the time pattern of rates with respect to the trend before and after partial deregulation, we plot the percent change in rates from year to year, $(\partial \log(r)/\partial t)*100$, in Fig. 1 for each commodity.[21] In all cases, there were very minimal and insignificant trends in the time rate of change in rates prior to partial deregulation. With the passage of Staggers in late 1980, there were very significant effects which dissipate with time for all commodities.

Specific interpretation of these results vary by commodity. Barley rates increased by 0.6% until 1981. In 1981, the rate of change was about −30% and has steadily fallen in magnitude with time. In 1995, the rate of change is about −12% per year. Similar patterns are observed for other commodities. For corn, sorghum, wheat, and soybeans, the pre-Staggers trend pointed to percent changes in rates per year of 1.6, 1.1, 0.3, and 1.5, respectively. The initial effect of partial deregulation on the time rate of change is uniformly negative with a −24, −37, −28, and −15% change per year (in 1981) for corn, sorghum, wheat, and soybeans. In 1995, again, the effects are smaller in magnitude for all commodities. The 1995 percent change in rates is −9, −15, −12, and −6% per year, respectively. These effects capture technological progress, changes in markups, and other variables in the trend. The results suggest such effects were not prevalent prior to partial deregulation and were quite substantial with the passage of Staggers, which while dissipating with time, remain quite strong.

The final set of results discussed are the effects of Staggers on rates as represented in Section 3. Using the estimates in Table 1, we illustrate these effects graphically, with Fig. 2 for each commodity. By construction, there are no regulatory effects prior to 1980. The effects of partial deregulation involve

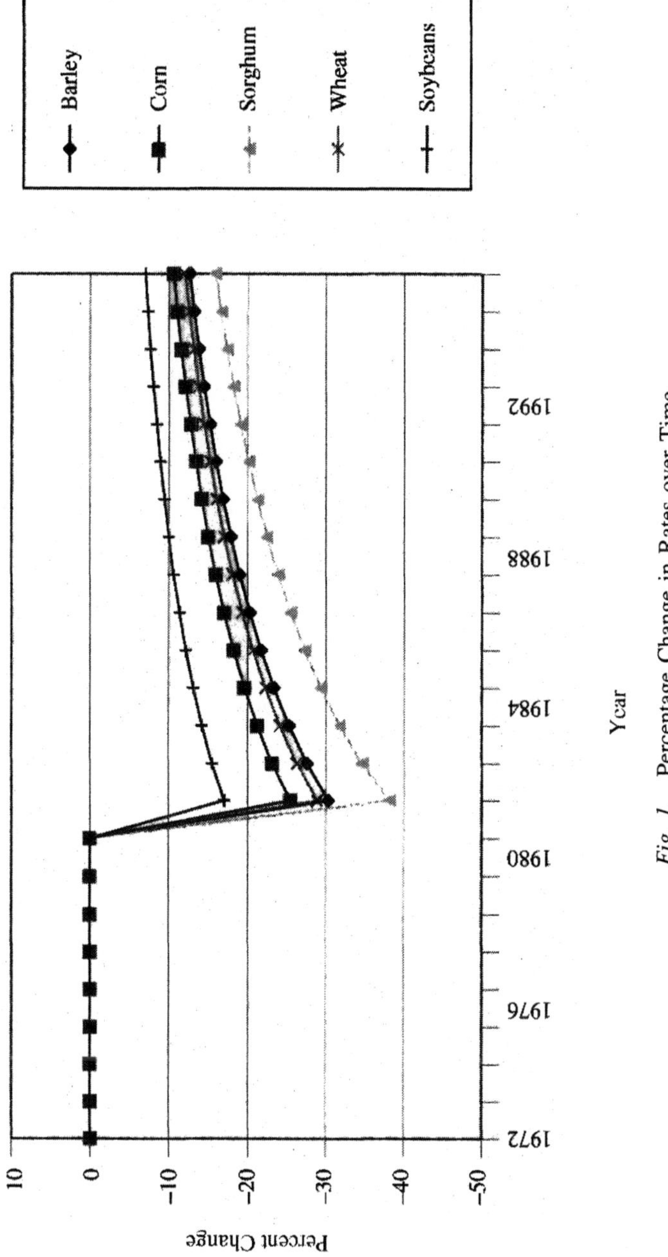

Fig. 1. Percentage Change in Rates over Time.

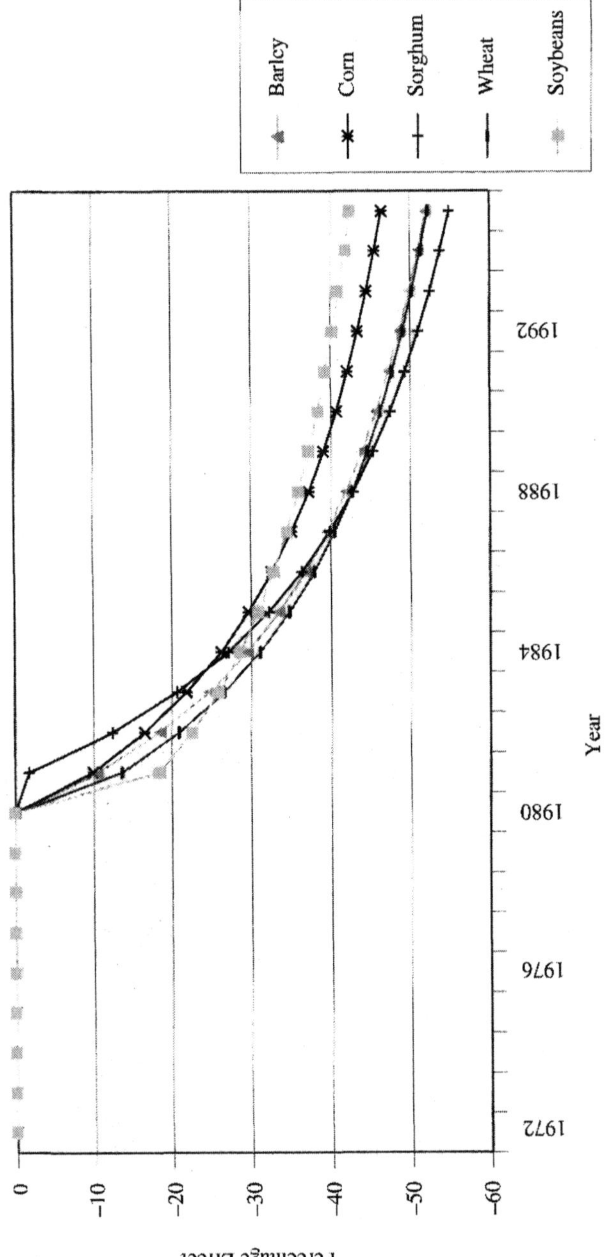

Fig. 2. The Percentage Effect of Partial Deregulation.

multiple parameters and is time dependent.[22] The effects are uniformly negative for all commodities in 1981. For barley, corn, sorghum, wheat, and soybeans the initial effect, i.e. the 1981 effect, is a −10.6, −9.9, −1.8, −13.7, and −18.4% change in rates, respectively. The initial effects of partial deregulation grew over time but at a decreasing rate. In 1995, the longer term percent reduction in rates are −52, −46, −55, −52, and −42 for barley, corn, sorghum, wheat, and soybeans, respectively. Both the figures and the estimates are consistent with priors. These results are consistent with the conjecture that partial deregulation has relatively small initial effects, but eventually converge to larger longer term effects.[23]

7. CONCLUSIONS

Partial deregulation of rail rates in grain has had an important effect on the evolution, efficiency, and conduct of the grain marketing industry. Several important features of the Staggers Rail Act (SRA) facilitated a change in the conduct of the rail shipping industry. Important SRA provisions induced selected line abandonment, mergers, development of short line railroads, and the introduction of numerous mechanisms to induce more efficient shipping practices and car allocation. The purpose of this study was to analyze the extent that observed changes in rail rates can be attributed to productivity changes and cost reductions, and to the more liberalized regulatory environment. This study developed an econometric model of shipping rates for grains through time. In particular, a model based on demand, costs, a pricing relation, and the regulatory regime was specified and estimated over the period 1972–1995 to identify the effect of these variables on rail rates.

Review of the data indicated a number of compelling facts. First, there have been both nominal and real reductions in rail rates since 1980. In particular, in the period prior to 1980, rail rates generally increased in real terms. However, in the period following the SRA, most rail rates decreased in real terms by 52% (ranging from 40–71% across commodities). Second, there has been a notable change in operating characteristics. Most important is the period following the SRA, when there were increases in tonmiles shipped, average length of haul, and average load per car along with decreases in miles of road operated. These variables affect equilibrium rate levels in several dimensions.

Results from the econometric analysis indicated that rate levels and their change through time are explained by these fundamental demand and cost factors. Several conclusions are drawn. First, commodity tonmiles affect rates negatively. Second, commodity prices affect rates positively, reflecting demand conditions. These results indicate that rates are sensitive to demand and are not entirely due to cost changes. Third, average length of haul (ALH) is an important variable affecting rates levels. In all cases, this variable was negative and significant. This is noteworthy, since during the post-SRA period, ALH has increased substantially, which resulted in a substantial reduction in rate levels.

The final set of results relate specifically to the effect of the partial deregulation instilled by the SRA. These results indicate that in general, in the period prior to SRA, productivity changes were non-existent. However, because of the SRA, there was a oneshot large improvement in productivity, and a concurrent reduction in rates. This was followed by continued productivity increases and rate reductions in the ensuing years. However, the effects dissipated, with most of the benefits realized after about ten years following partial deregulation. The initial effect of partial deregulation resulted in rate reductions ranging from 2 to 19%. However, by 1995, these cumulative effects resulted in rate reductions ranging from −42 to −55% relative to the rate level which would have been realized without a change in the regulatory regime.

ACKNOWLEDGMENTS

The authors gratefully acknowledge the contributions of Mark Burton and Bruce Dahl in this research as well research support from the *Organization for Western Economic Cooperation*. Demcey Johnson and John Bitzan provided constructive comments. However, errors and omissions are the responsibility of the authors.

NOTES

1. While considerably deregulated, firms in the industry remain subject to price, network, and market structure regulations. Partial deregulation also eased merger guidelines and abandonment. The former has led to a dramatic reduction in the number of firms, while the latter has led to a dramatic reduction in the size (density) of the network operated by the Class I railroad industry.

2. The effects of partial deregulation are often captured in an intercept dummy which can be interpreted as an instantaneous adjustment to a new long-run rate. A linear adjustment factor (i.e. an intercept dummy with a time interaction) allows rates to adjust over time but usually lead to inconsistent out-of-sample predictions. In contrast, our treatment allows rates to adjust initially but the effects enter non-linearly and allow the long-term effect of partial deregulation to be inferred from the data.

3. In addition to these studies, there are several other studies, e.g. Babcock (1981, 1984), Sorenson (1984), and Babcock et al. (1985), that provide descriptions of various aspects of partial deregulation on grain handling and shipping.

4. Atkinson and Kerkvliet (1986) and Friedlaender (1992) examine coal rates. Atkinson and Kerkvliet find rents associated with coal movement increased under partial deregulation. Friedlaender calculated markups, finding that regulation was constraining in some coal markets but not in others, affecting firms and commodities asymmetrically.

She also suggested that it was likely that market power of railroads increased in transportation markets for manufactured and agricultural goods.

5. Generally, rates are the result of market dominant forces if the revenue to variable cost ratio was greater than a threshold (now 180%) and there was a lack of effective intramodal, intermodal, product and geographic competition. See Eaton and Center (1985) and Wilson (1996) for further discussion.

6. There are a number of studies discussing contracts. See, for example, Schmitz and Fuller (1995), MacDonald and Cavalluzzo (1996), and Klindworth, Sorenson, Babcock and Chow 1985).

7. *Milling and Baking News*, Sept. 30, 1997, p. 19.

8. *Milling and Baking News*, Sept. 19, 1997 p. 15.

9. Wilson (1998) provides a detailed description of the evolution of car allocation systems in the United States. Wilson and Priewe (1997) analyze the implications of these mechanisms on grain trading strategies using stochastic dynamic simulation, and Wilson and Dahl (1997) analyze the bidding strategies and implications of these mechanisms.

10. An ideal approach to estimating the effects of partial deregulation would be to estimate demands, costs, and pricing relationships simultaneously using a systems approach e.g. three-stage-least squares. Owing to data difficulties as well as the difficulties of multiple demands network technologies of railroads, such an approach is not tractable. Conceptually, there is a separate demand for each price in the network, a multiple output cost function allowing for differences in costs for each of the outputs, and a separate pricing relation for each of the outputs. As most rail markets are quite extensive, such an approach is intractable.

11. Such a framework has been used to examine rail rates e.g. Wilson (1994) as well as motor carrier markets e.g. Ying and Keeler (1991) and Nebesky and McMullen (1995).

12. Equation (3) follows most of the similar specifications in the literature. A possible difficulty with estimation of Eq. (3) by least squares is the possibility that the solution of the demand, cost, pricing, and regulatory regime equations for prices may have variables on the right-hand side that are potentially endogenous, and, as a result, may introduce a source of bias. We treat the issue of whether treating such variables as exogenous imparts bias on the least squares estimates as an empirical issue.

13. The use of an aggregate rate is quite common in related studies. See Boyer (1987), McFarland (1989), and Barnekov and Kliet (1990) each of whom analyze rates aggregated across all dimensions including not only origin-destination but also commodity. Also, Burton (1993) and Wilson (1994) analyze aggregate rates of various commodities. Finally, there are a few studies that focus on relatively disaggregate commodity and geographic levels. See, for example, Fuller et al. (1987), Wilson et al. (1988), and MacDonald (1989).

14. The percentage of unit train traffic, average shipment size, and/or the percentage of bulk traffic are variables that often appear in rate regressions of the form appearing above. In each case, these variables at the system level have increased over time and, in particular, since partial deregulation. At the individual commodity level, such variables are not available. These variables are likely captured in the intercepts and in the time trends as discussed below.

15. See Wolfe (1991) and Wolfe and Linde (1997) for a detailed explanation of these data. We note that the waybill sample has been subject to criticisms and defenses. The waybill prior to 1981 may underrepresent multiple car movements, actual rates and

reported rates may differ due to rules of disclosure with contracts, tons per car may be measured with error due to the use of billed rather than actual weights, and the Freight Mandatory Rule 11 results in rebilling of railroad movements and may result in shipment distance being understated and tons per carload being overstated. In grain markets, the underrepresentation of multiple car rates are ameliorated due to the innovations occurring primarily after 1981 and the use of the expanded waybill records rather than the individual records. As such, many of the difficulties are ameliorated. The remaining difficulties have largely been discussed elsewhere and, while potentially problematic, previous research does not suggest they are tantamount. See, for example, MacDonald (1987, 1989).

16. We explored a variety of deflators and report those based on the AAR's index of labor, fuel and materials, and supplies combined index. We also estimated the model with the producer price index for finished goods and the GNP price deflator. In both cases, neither the qualitative or numerical results were materially affected. We use the AAR deflated results because of the fact that the estimated model is based on a markup equation with homogenous of degree one marginal costs. Factoring the changes in the factor price component provides a natural deflator. We further note that placing the deflator as a right-hand side variable in most cases results in a coefficient not statistically different from 1.

17. In terms of the timing of the initial effects of Staggers, we examined alternative switching points for the regulatory regime as well as alternative smoothing techniques (e.g. defining the dummy variable with increasing weights such as STAG = 0.2 for 1980, STAG = 0.6 for 1981, STAG = 0.9 for 1982, etc.) The qualitative and numerical results are not materially affected, and given our smoothing technique above, we use a STAG dummy variable to capture the change in regulatory regimes. In all cases, the models fit the data so well that they provide little discrimination between the models. However, the simulated effects of a change in regulatory regime provide support for the effects of Staggers. For example, if STAG is defined with 1980 instead of 1981 as the switching point, the initial effects of STAG is almost uniformly positive. If STAG is defined with 1982 as the switching effect the effects are substantially larger than those reported. While the regulatory effects of the smoothed dummy (STAG with varying weights) are quite comparable to those reported, the effects of a change in regulatory regime on the time-related effects $\partial \log(\text{rate})/\partial t$ have quite large negative effects in 1980 and 1981, reversing quickly in 1982. The behavior of the time effects reported later with the usual STAG switch point is much more realistic and vies for the specification reported.

18. Average load is simply tonmiles divided by the number of carmiles. Such a variable is probably not as useful as shipment size in explaining rate changes. In the data, we attempted to proxy average shipment size with tons divided by the sample size (the number of waybills on which the statistics are based). We did not obtain significant effects, and the measure was "noisy".

19. When we do not include these variables in the regression; the effect of STAG and the asymptotic adjustment to STAG is larger than when we control for these variables. The differences range from 4% to 24% in magnitude.

20. This conclusion is tempered somewhat by the failure to separately identify changes in marginal costs from changes in markups. The finding described here is consistent with significant technological progress (reducing rates) that offset increases in the markup term if the latter is present.

21. In our calculations, we include only the parameter effect. That is, we exclude from the discussion and graphs, the effects operating through the righthand side variables. These were discussed previously and their inclusion rests on a reasonable model generating their dynamic behavior.

22. The results reported contain the effects of AL, USTONMI, and MOR operating through the correlations with the trend and Staggers dummy variable. The effect of not estimating the parameters of these coefficients to separately identify the effect impacts the figures reported. Calculating the effects given by the above equation but using the Appendix specification i.e. washing out the effects of AL, USTONMI, and MOR, yields 1981 and 1995 effects for barley of −4.9 and −64.5%, for corn of −2.3 and −46.6, for sorghum of +4.1 and −41.6%, for wheat of −13.3 and −55.4%, and for soybeans of −15.9 and −50.7%. Generally, removing the effects of these three variables from both the initial effects and the long-run effects tempers the effects of Staggers operating through both the dummy and the trend variable.

23. As noted earlier, these results are qualitatively equivalent and numerically similar to results obtained by excluding commodity tonmiles from the specification. Inclusion of effects operating through righthand side variables (using a time trend with a Stagger's dummy and interaction) again yields qualitatively equivalent but numerically different results for both the specification in the text as well as in the Appendix.

REFERENCES

Adam, B. D., & Anderson, D. G. (1985). Implications of the Staggers Rail Act of 1980 for the Level and Variability of Country Elevator Price Bids. *Proceedings of the Transportation Research Forum, 26*, 357–363.

Atkinson, S. E., & Kerkvliet, J. (1986). Measuring the Multilateral Allocation of Rents: Wyoming Low Sulfur Coal. *Rand Journal of Economics, 17*, 416–430.

Babcock, M. W. (1981). Potential Impact of Rail Deregulation in the Kansas Wheat Market. *Journal of Economics*, 7, 93–98.

Babcock, M. W. (1984). *Efficiency and Adjustment: The Impact of Railroad Deregulation.* Cato Institute, Washington D.C.

Babcock, M. W., Sorenson, L. O., Chow, M. H., & Klindworth, K. A. (1985). Impact of the Staggers Rail Act on Agriculture: A Kansas Case Study. *Proceedings of the Transportation Research Forum, 26*, 364–372.

Barnekov, C. C., & Kleit, A. N. (1990). The Efficiency Effects of Railroad Deregulation in the United States. *International Journal of Transport Economics, 17*, 21–36.

Berndt, E. R., Friedlaender, A. F., Chiang, J. S. W., & Vellturo, C. A. (1993). Cost Effects of Mergers and Deregulation in the U.S. Rail Industry. *Journal of Productivity Analysis, 4*, 127–144.

Boyer, K. D. (1987). The Cost of Price Regulation: Lessons from Railroad Deregulation. *Rand Journal of Economics, 18*, 408–416.

Bresnahan, T. (1989). Empirical Studies of Industries with Market Power. In: R. Schmalensee & R. D. Willig (Eds), *Handbook of Industrial Organization.* Elsevier Science Publishing Company: Amsterdam.

Burton, M. L. (1993). Railroad Deregulation, Carrier Behavior, and Shipper Response: A Disaggregated Analysis. *Journal of Regulatory Economics, 5*, 417–434.

Eaton, J. A., & Center, J. A. (1985). A Tale of Two Markets: The ICC's Use of Product and

Geographic Competition in the Assessment of Rail Market Dominance. *Transportation Practitioners Journal, 53*, 16–35.

Friedlaender, A. F. (1992). Coal Rates and Revenue Adequacy in a Quasi-Regulated Rail Industry. *Rand Journal of Economics, 23*, 376–394.

Fuller, S., Bessler, D., MacDonald, J., & Wohlgenant, M. (1987). Effect of Deregulation on Export-Grain Rates in the Plains and Corn Belt. *Journal of the Transportation Research Forum, 28*, 160–167.

Fuller, S., Makus, L., & Taylor, M. (1983). Effect of Railroad Deregulation in Export Grain Rates. *North Central Journal of Agricultural Economics*, 51–62.

Fuller, S., & Shanmugham, C. (1981). Effectiveness of Competition to Limit Rail Increases under Deregulation: The Case of Wheat Exports from the Southern Plains. *Southern Journal of Agricultural Economics, 13*, 11–19.

Hauser, R. J. (1986). Competitive Forces in the U.S. Inland Grain Transportation Industry: A Regional Perspective. *The Logistics and Transportation Review, 22*, 158–173.

Hausman, J. A. (1978). Specification Tests in Econometrics. *Econometrica, 46*, 1251–1271.

Klindworh, K., Sorenson, O., Babcock, M., & Chow, M. (1985). Impacts of Rail Deregulation on Marketing of Kansas Wheat., USDA, Office of Transportation.

Levin, R. (1981). Railroad Rates, Profitability, and Welfare under Deregulation. *The Bell Journal of Economics, 12*, 1–26.

MacDonald, J. M. (1987). Competition and Rail Rates for the Shipment of Corn, Soybeans, and Wheat. *Rand Journal of Economics, 18*, 151–163.

MacDonald, J. M. (1989). Railroad Deregulation, Innovation, and Competition: Effects of the Staggers Act on Grain Transportation. *Journal of Law and Economics, 32*, 63–95.

MacDonald, J. M., & Cavalluzzo, L. C. (1996). Railroad Deregulation: Pricing Reforms, Shipper Responses, and the Effects on Labor. *Industrial and Labor Relations Review, 50*, 80–91.

McFarland, H. (1989). The Effects of United States Railroad Deregulation on Shippers, Labor, and Capital. *Journal of Regulatory Economics, 1*, 259–270.

National Grain and Feed Association (1997). Statement at the Public Hearing on *Status of Rail Freight Service in the Western United States*. STB Ex Parte No. 573, Oct. 27.

National Grain and Feed Association (1998). Statement before the Subcommittee on Surface Transportation and Merchant Marine, Committee on Commerce, Science and Transportation, U.S. Senate.

Nebesky, W., McMullen, B. S., & Lee, M. (1995). Testing for Market Power in the U.S. Motor Carrier Industry. *Review of Industrial Organization, 10*, 559–576.

Priewe, S., & Wilson, W. (1997). *Forward Shipping Options for Grain By Rail: A Strategic Risk Analysis*. Agricultural Economics Report No. 372, Department of Agricultural Economics, North Dakota State University, Fargo, March 1997.

Schmitz, J., & Fuller, S. W. (1995). Effect of Contract Disclosure on Railroad Grain Rates: An Analysis of Corn Belt Corridors. *The Logistics and Transportation Review, 3*, 97–124.

Sorenson, L. O. (1984). Some Impacts of Rail Regulatory Changes on Grain Industries. *American Journal of Agricultural Economics, 66*, 645–650.

Thompson, S. R., Hauser, R., & Coughlin, B. (1990). The Competitiveness of Rail Rates on Export Bound Grain. *The Logistics and Transportation Review, 26*, 3552.

Vellturo, C. A., Berndt, E. R., Friedlaender, A. F., Chiang, J. S. W., & Showalter, M. H. (1992). Deregulation, Mergers, and Cost Savings in Class I Railroads. *Journal of Economics and Management Strategy, 1*, 339–369.

Wilson, W. W. (1994). Market Specific Effects of Rail Deregulation. *Journal of Industrial Economics, 42*, 1–22.

Wilson, W. W. (1996). Legislated Market Dominance. *Research in Transportation Economics, 4*, 449–467.
Wilson, W. W. (1997). Cost Savings and Productivity in the Railroad Industry. *Journal of Regulatory Economics, 11*, 21–40.
Wilson, W. W. (1998). *U.S. Grain Handling and Transportation System: Factors Contributing to the Dynamic Changes in the 1980s and 1990s*. Agricultural Economics Report, Department of Agricultural Economics, North Dakota State University, Fargo, ND.
Wilson, W. W., Wilson, W. W., & Koo, W. W. (1988). Modal Competition and Pricing in Grain Transport. *Journal of Transport Economics and Policy, 22*, 319–337.
Wilson, W. W., & Dahl, B. (1997). *Bidding on Railcars for Grain: A Strategic Analysis*. Agricultural Economics Report No. 376, Department of Agricultural Economics, North Dakota State University, Fargo, ND, May 1997.
Wilson, W. W., & Priewe, S. (1998). *Railcar Allocation Mechanisms For Grain: A Comparison Among U.S. Class I Railroads*. Agricultural Economics Report, Department of Agricultural Economics, North Dakota State University, Fargo, September 1998.
Wilson, W., Priewe, S., & Dahl, B. (1998). Forward Shipping Options for Grain by Rail: A Strategic Risk Analysis. *Journal of Agricultural and Resource Economics, 23*, 1–19.
Winston, C. (1998). U.S. Industry Adjustment to Economic Deregulation. *Journal of Economic Perspectives, 12*, 89–110.
Wolfe, E. (1991). The Carload Way bill Statistics: A Content Analysis. *Journal of the Transport Research Forum, 32*.
Wolfe, K. E., & Linde, W. (1997). The Carload Waybill Statistics: Usefulness For Economic Analysis. *Journal of the Transportation Research Forum, 26*, 26–41.
Ying, J. S., & Keeler, T. E. (1991). Pricing in a Deregulated Environment. *The Rand Journal of Economics, 22*, 264–273.

APPENDIX

Table A.1. Fully Specified Regression Results by Commodity.

	Commodity				
	Barley	Corn	Sorghum	Wheat	Soybeans
Constant	13.24	−7.59	−42.24*	9.57	−3.87
	(1.41)	(0.76)	(2.73)	(0.53)	(−0.30)
Commodity Ton Miles	−0.04	−0.11	−0.01	−0.17	−0.16
	(0.50)	(0.96)	(.07)	(1.16)	(1.23)
Commodity Price	0.09	0.14*	0.06	0.06	0.09
	(1.5)	(2.37)	(0.62)	(0.59)	(0.64)
Avg. Length of Haul	−0.64*	−0.64*	−1.03*	−0.63*	−0.67*
	(4.09)	(2.59)	(3.60)	(2.13)	(2.78)
SRA	17.54*	10.76*	10.34*	11.71*	9.37*
	(6 01)	(4.05)	(1.81)	(1.80)	(2.26)
Pre-Staggers Trend	0.01	−0.01	0.03	0.01	0.01
	(0.74)	(.48)	(1.51)	(0.08)	(0.12)
Post-Staggers Trend	−19.35*	−11.87*	−11.33*	−13.04*	−10.49*
	(6.00)	(4.08)	(1.83)	(1.81)	(2.30)
US Ton Mi	−0.27	0.68*	1.03	−0.07	0.47
	(0.89)	(2.89)	(1.44)	(0.17)	(1.34)
MOR	−0.70	−0.29	−2.14*	−0.48	−0.15
	(1.18)	(0.47)	(2.47)	(0.37)	(0.16)
AL	−1.01*	−0.09	0.11	−0.65	−0.39
	(2.00)	(0.21)	(0.19)	(0.94)	(0.77)
Adj R^2	0.99	0.99	0.98	0.98	0.98
DW	2.23	2.16	1.91	1.55	1.93

Values in ( ) are the t-statistic and * indicates significance at the 10% level.

MEASURING TECHNOLOGICAL CHANGE IN THE U.S. MOTOR CARRIER INDUSTRY

Lawrence Wong

ABSTRACT

This paper re-examines the impact of deregulation and technological change on U.S. motor carrier costs for the period 1976–1987. A truncated, third-order translog cost function, developed by Stevenson (1980) allows us to decompose technological change into three components: input bias, output bias, and characteristics bias. We examine the source of these biases and use the model to test the Schumpeter hypothesis, which asserts that large firms innovate at a faster rate than small firms. We show that technological change has been labor-saving and purchased capital-using, and that these input biases were induced by changes in output level. The increase in the capital cost share and the decrease in fuel cost share are attributed to deregulation. Over time, the LTL sector of the motor carrier industry has become more capital intensive, resulting in even higher entry barriers. The output bias of technological change on the representative firm is not significant and our results do not support the Schumpeter hypothesis in the LTL sector of the motor carrier industry. Technological change has increased the economies of larger shipment size over time, but has not significantly altered the impact

Transportation After Deregulation, Volume 6, pages 25–54.
2001 by Elsevier Science Ltd.
ISBN: 0-7623-0780-3

of average load, average length of haul, or insurance per ton-mile on costs over time. Also we find that deregulation, through its negative impact on technological change, has resulted in higher industry costs.

1. INTRODUCTION

The passage of the Motor Carrier Act in 1980 led to many studies assessing the impact of deregulation on the motor carrier industry. However, few studies have explicitly examined the relationship between technical change and deregulation. As the industry concentration has increased substantially in the less-than-truckload (LTL) sector after deregulation, policy makers have become concerned with the potential for oligopolistic pricing behavior. If, however, technological change is the driving force behind the increase in industry concentration, then policymakers need to weigh the benefits of technological advance against the social costs associated with oligopolistic pricing.

According to Hicks (1932), technological change is considered as neutral if the marginal rate of technical substitution between each pair of inputs is independent of technical change. However, technological change may be biased toward input and/or output. If technical change is biased toward input, then factor-cost shares will change and this will have an impact on factor income distribution. If technical change is biased toward output, the minimum efficient firm size will be altered and this will have implications for the degree of competition supportable in the industry.

Schumpeter (1962) argues that "perfect competition may be a perfectly suitable vehicle for static resource allocation, but the large firm operating in a concentrated market is the most powerful engine of progress." If true, this challenges the conventional wisdom regarding the unfavorable outcomes from monopoly.

The purpose of this paper is to re-examine the effects of deregulation on technological change in the LTL sector of the trucking industry using a panel of 126 firms between 1976 and 1987. The sources of technological change are examined using a methodology developed by Stevenson (1980). In particular, we estimate a translog cost function with a truncated third-order Taylor series expansion time trend from which the source of technological bias can be extracted as explained below.

The organization of this paper is as follows. The next section provides a brief regulatory background of the trucking industry and summarizes some of the major results of industry deregulation. The econometric model is then specified and the data are described. The major results are then presented followed by a discussion of their policy implications.

2. REGULATORY AND DEREGULATION BACKGROUND

Motor carrier regulation began in 1935 when Congress passed the Motor Carrier Act and gave the Interstate Commerce Commission (ICC) the authority to regulate the industry. A primary goal of this act was to protect the regulated railroads from trucking competition and to ensure a stable transportation system. Federal economic regulations imposed by the ICC consisted of minimum rate, entry and operating restrictions.

Rate regulation referred to the ability of the ICC to set minimum, maximum, and actual rates. Entry restrictions took the form of certificates of public convenience and necessity. Potential entrants had to prove to the satisfaction of the ICC both that the service was needed and that they were "fit, willing, and able" to serve the public. Finally, the ICC placed restrictions on the operating rights of motor carriers, controlling both routes and commodities carried. These restrictions limited the scope of competition amongst motor carriers and had potential impacts on operating efficiency.

Economic theory suggests that regulations such as price controls and entry restrictions distort economic behavior and lead to resource misallocation, welfare loss, and inefficiencies. Many studies have asserted that ICC regulation of motor carriers impeded economic efficiency and permitted prices to rise above competitive level. Boyer (1993) asserts that another important consequence of rate regulation, though hard to measure, was to discourage service innovation. To prevent costly quality competition and to support rate regulation, the ICC forbid service offerings with performance guarantees and with rebates in the event that a carrier did not deliver a shipment as promised. Boyer argues that without performance guarantees, just-in-time inventory methods were impossible; hence, rate regulation was incompatible with just-in-time inventory methods for modern manufacturing. Thus regulation was believed to distort the competitive equilibrium leading to the misallocation of resources, higher operating costs and price, lower productivity growth and slower technological innovation.

Substantial deregulation occurred in the trucking industry with the passage of the Motor Carrier Act (MCA) of 1980. The MCA largely deregulated rates and entry requirements, and lifted commodity and route restrictions. Proponents of deregulation predicted that prices would fall, productivity would improve, concentration would decline, and a competitive industry equilibrium would emerge. Here it is important to distinguish between the truckload (TL) and the less-than-truckload (LTL) sectors of the industry. Economists who promoted deregulation presumed that the entire motor carrier industry had relatively insignificant barriers to entry, utilized relatively low technology in terms of equipment and labor skills, and possessed no economies of scale. This is an accurate depiction of the TL sector of the industry since a TL carrier picks up a large volume shipment (often filling an entire trailer), and carries it directly to the final destination without reloading. Because TL traffic does not go through terminals, the economic barriers to entry in the TL sector are very low and the operating process is quite simple.

In contrast, a LTL carrier depends on a distribution system involving a multitude of trucks stopping at numerous consignors, taking on small shipments, aggregating them at a central terminal facility, and consolidating them into large shipments for long-distance transport to a remote terminal facilities, where they are disassembled and put on small trucks to be distributed to their individual consignees. In order to provide nationwide service, a LTL carrier requires a large network involving many terminals. In addition, sophisticated information technology and skilled personnel are needed to manage and schedule the line-haul, pick up, and delivery operations. Therefore, large scale LTL operation is a very complex business requiring substantial capital investment, extensive computer and telecommunications technology, and a highly skilled labor force. For these reasons, the barriers to entry in the LTL sector are high, and consequently, the economic impact of deregulation on TL and LTL sectors of the motor carrier industry turned out to be quite different.

According to Glaskowsky (1990), nearly 20,000 carriers entered the trucking industry by 1987. However, the vast majority of these were small TL carriers with just one, two or a few trucks. The large number of new entrants into the TL sector produced intense price competition and, as a result, TL rates fell and have remained very competitive. Because of the absence of barriers to entry in the TL sector, the massive entry of TL carriers was well predicted by deregulators and the results were close to the classical economic definition of monopolistic competition. In contrast, the market structure in the LTL sector is almost exactly the opposite of that in the TL sector after deregulation. As the ICC granted broader operating certificates and allowed service to be performed over any available route, large LTL carriers began positioning themselves in the deregulated environment by increasing network of terminals and expanding into newly acquired territories. For example, during the first twelve months following the MCA, Consolidated Freightways added 42 terminals while Yellow Freight added 100 even though recession-level traffic might be inadequate to cover the higher fixed costs.[1] Table 1 shows the number of the terminals for the big three LTL carriers in 1980 and 1989.[2]

As competition intensified following deregulation, many medium and small LTL carriers went out of business, but there were no successful new entrants

Table 1. Number of Terminals.

Carriers	1980	1989
Consolidated Freightways, Inc.	330	667
Roadway Express, Inc.	449	602
Yellow Freight System, Inc.	248	640

into the LTL sector. Leaseway Express was the only major carrier that entered the LTL sector of the industry after deregulation and it left the market in early 1985 with losses between $5 and $10 million.[3] Therefore, what developed after deregulation was sharply increased concentration in the LTL sector and less concentration in the TL sector.

To understand how the market structure of the LTL sector has evolved, Table 2 shows the concentration ratios and the Herfindahl-Hirschman Index[4] (HHI) for the ICC Instruction 27 carriers[5] based on the total operating revenues. The concentration ratio is the percentage of the industry's revenues accounted for by the largest 4 and largest 8 firms. In general, the higher the concentration ratio, the less competitive the industry is. The HHI is another measurement of industry concentration frequently reviewed by the U.S. Department of Justice for antitrust policy analysis and it is based on sum of squares of each firm's market share.

As shown in Table 2, the four-firm and eight-firm concentration ratios for the LTL sector doubled between 1976 and 1987. Due to failures and mergers, the number of firms at the end of 1987 declined to less than half of the number in 1976. Over the years, the market structure in the LTL sector became more oligopolistic than monopolistic. Although still below the Federal threshold for a moderately concentrated industry, the large rise of the HHI does reflect the increasingly uneven distribution of the market shares over time. Notably, the top three firms gained substantial market shares at the expense of the smaller firms, dominating the market during the 12-year period. Figure 1 shows the market shares of the three dominant LTL firms over time.

Increases in concentration may occur because of normal adjustments to economies of scale and scope, as well from predatory pricing and other unfair business practices. As concentration in the LTL sector continues to rise and many LTL trucking companies confine their operations to particular regions of the country, the potential for oligopolistic pricing behavior is of concern to policy makers. If efficient producers were driven out of the market by predatory pricing and the LTL sector of the trucking industry evolves into a collusive oligopoly, some form of re-regulation may be necessary. However, if high

Table 2. LTL Operating Revenue Concentration 1976–1987.

	1976	1977	1978	1979	1980	1981	1982	1983	1984	1985	1986	1987
4-firm ratio	0.17	0.18	0.19	0.21	0.21	0.23	0.28	0.30	0.32	0.32	0.33	0.37[a]
8-firm ratio	0.24	0.26	0.27	0.30	0.32	0.34	0.38	0.40	0.43	0.43	0.45	0.49
HHI	127	145	154	176	194	215	266	298	343	347	372	460
No. of firms	614	552	610	565	498	418	386	361	326	332	312	273

[a] According to Glaskowsky (1990), the 4-firm concentration ratio in 1987 reached 65% if one included the $8 billion annual revenue of United Parcel Services Company.

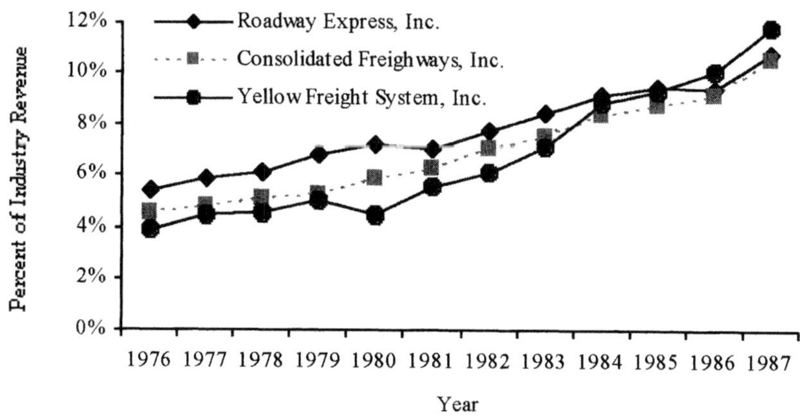

Fig. 1. Market Share of LTL Sector.

concentration was due to adjustments to economies of scale and efficiency gains from expansion of terminal networks, and dominant LTL carriers pass on the cost savings to customers, then there is no rationale for any form of antitrust action.

The increase in industry concentration has attracted tremendous attention from transportation economists and there have been many studies of the effects of the MCA on the motor carrier industry. Most of the studies focus on pricing behavior in a deregulated environment and whether deregulation has led to reductions in cost. Keeler (1986) estimates a translog cost function for a panel of twelve firms from 1966–1983 and finds that costs increased as a result of deregulation. Winston et al. (1990) use compensating variations to estimate the value that shippers place on changes in rates and service quality attributable to deregulation. Their results show that deregulation has caused a reduction in rates and an improvement in service quality. However, in contrast to its impact on the TL sector, deregulation has caused the total costs in the LTL sector to rise.

Ying and Keeler (1991) analyze the impact of deregulation on truck rates over the period 1980–1983 and 1980–1985 based on a rate equation and cost function. Their results show that rates fell by 25–35% by 1985 as a result of deregulation. Nebesky et al. (1995) employ new empirical industrial organization techniques to determine whether monopoly pricing behavior exists in the more concentrated LTL sector using cross-sectional data between 1977 and 1988. Their estimates of price-cost margins indicate that regulation-induced market power existed prior to deregulation, and that the increase in industry concentration is not due to anti-competitive pricing behavior, but they give no detailed explanations for the observed increase in concentration.

Other studies provide evidence of economies of scale and suggest that the low levels of concentration prior to 1980 were the result of regulation rather than the lack of scale economies. Kling (1990) attributes the rapid growth of LTL firms after deregulation to economies of size. He tests for a relationship between size and market share by regressing the annual change in market share of large LTL firms on current market share and on time dummy variables over the period from 1978 to 1987. His results show that large LTL firms are able to offer lower rates and have significant advantage in gaining market shares after deregulation. Therefore, deregulation appears to have given these large national LTL firms a competitive edge over the small LTL firms, contributing to the increase in concentration. Ying (1990a) analyzes the effect of regulatory reform on technical change using cross-sectional data of 1975, 1980, and 1984. His results suggest that returns to scale have increased following deregulation.

Ying (1990b) analyzes the effect of deregulation on productivity growth using panel data from 1975 to 1984. He captures productivity growth and regulatory impacts by including a time trend and a deregulation dummy variable in a translog cost function. His first-order estimate of time trend is negative but statistically insignificant. Viewing the time trend as a measure of normal productivity change, he concludes that there is no productivity growth or decline at the sample mean. His first-order estimate of deregulation variable is 0.56083 and is significant at 1% level; however, he does not interpret this to mean that deregulation had a positive effect on cost. He argues that the impact of deregulation on the cost of a representative firm should be simulated using the sample mean of all variables in each year from 1980–1984. Using the simulated results, he shows that deregulation raised cost by 7.25% the first year, perhaps due to adjustment costs and thereafter cost declined annually resulting in cost savings of 22.84% by 1984.

More recently, McMullen and Okuyama (2000) examine the productivity changes in the trucking industry between 1977 and 1990 using a Malmquist Index approach. The authors decompose the productivity changes into changes in technical efficiency and changes in technology. Their results indicate that firms appear to have increased their technical efficiency in the post MCA periods, but this was offset by what appears to be technological regression resulting in no overall productivity improvement following deregulation.

McMullen and Lee (1999) examine efficiency changes before and after deregulation using a stochastic frontier approach. They estimate twelve individual cost frontiers (1976–1987) for the LTL sector of the industry and find that average industry inefficiency was between 14 and 27% for the entire period, with deregulation having no significant impact on inefficiency at the industry level. Using a tobit model to regress the estimated firm specific inefficiency on a set of firm characteristics, the authors find that union firms were 1.5% less efficient than non-union firms in the pre-MCA years and about 4% less efficient in the post-MCA years. The widening of inefficiency gap after deregulation suggests that non-union firms have been able to take advantage of increased operating flexibility to move closer to their cost/production frontiers while union firms may still be subject to many union rules that impede efficiency. These studies, however, do not address the sources of technological bias nor the Schumpeter hypothesis.

3. ECONOMETRIC MODEL

In order to examine technological bias and the Schumpeter hypothesis, we follow Stevenson (1980) and specify a translog cost function with a time trend incorporated as a truncated third-order Taylor series expansion. This specification has several advantages over the standard second-order translog approximation used in Ying (1990a, b), although at a cost of adding more coefficients to be estimated. When the time trend is approximated by a second-order Taylor expansion, the parameters on the second-order terms are assumed to be constant over time; hence the source of the technological bias and the Schumpeter hypothesis cannot be addressed. A truncated third-order approximation allows the second order coefficients to vary over time, so we can explicitly test whether changes in technology are biased toward input, output, or firm attributes, and also the source of the technological bias. For example, if technical change is relatively i th factor using (causes a firm to increase input *i*), we can further test whether this input bias is driven by changes in input prices, output, or a firm's characteristics.

The general translog cost function can be expressed as

$$\ln C = \ln C\ (y, \mathbf{p}, \mathbf{a}, T, D) + \varepsilon \tag{1}$$

where C represents long-run total cost, y represents ton-miles, **p** represents a vector of input prices, a represents a vector of firm attributes, T represents time trend, and D is a deregulation variable. All variables except D and T are normalized by their sample mean. The time trend, defined as year minus 1975, is viewed as a technological variable and should capture the effect of productivity growth on the cost function. The deregulation variable, D, takes on the value of 0 for 1976–1979 and the value of 1 for 1980–1987. The random error term, ε, is assumed to have a normal distribution, capturing the effect of random disturbances which are beyond the control of the firm. A translog cost function is selected because it is a flexible functional form that allows substitution among factors of production, scale economies to be unrestricted, and enables explicit testing of the technology structure. Using a cost function approach to capture technology presumes that the firms being examined are efficient and therefore cannot address the issue of inefficiency. The estimating equation is written as follows:

$$\begin{aligned}\ln C = {} & \beta_0 + \beta_y \ln y + 1/2\, \beta_{yy} (\ln y)^2 + \Sigma_i \beta_i \ln P_i + \Sigma_j \beta_j \ln a_j + \Sigma_i \beta_{iy} \ln P_i \ln y \\ & + \Sigma_j \beta_{jy} \ln a_j \ln y + \Sigma_i \Sigma_j \beta_{ij} \ln P_i \ln a_j + 1/2\, \Sigma_i \Sigma_m \beta_{im} \ln P_i \ln P_m \\ & + 1/2\, \Sigma_j \Sigma_n \beta_{jn} \ln a_j \ln a_n \\ & + \{\beta_T T + \beta_{TT}\, 1/2\, T^2 + \Sigma_i \beta_{Ti} T \ln P_i + 1/2\, \Sigma_i \Sigma_m \beta_{Tim} T \ln P_i \ln P_m + \beta_{Ty} T \ln y \\ & + 1/2\, \beta_{Tyy} T (\ln y)^2 + \Sigma_i \beta_{Tiy} T \ln P_i \ln y + \Sigma_j \beta_{Tj} T \ln a_j \\ & + \Sigma_i \Sigma_j \beta_{Tij} T \ln P_i \ln a_j + \Sigma_j \beta_{Tjy} T \ln a_j \ln y + 1/2\, \Sigma_j \Sigma_n \beta_{Tjn} T \ln a_j \ln a_n \} \\ & + \{\beta_D D + \beta_{DT} D\, T + \beta_{Dy} D \ln y + \Sigma_j \beta_{Dj} D \ln a_j + \Sigma_i \beta_{Di} D \ln P_i \} + \varepsilon \qquad (2)\end{aligned}$$

where the indices i and m pertain to input prices, j and n to attributes, y to output, T to time, and D to deregulation. The variables within the first pair of brackets represent the time trend terms. The variables within the second pair of brackets represent the set of additional terms to capture the impact of the MCA passed in 1980. The source of the technological bias, if exists, is captured by the the parameter estimates of the third order terms, β_{Tij}, β_{Tim}, β_{Tjn}, β_{Tiy}, β_{Tjy} and β_{Tyy}.

The assumption of cost minimization implies that the ith input's cost share can be obtained by Shephard's lemma:

$$\begin{aligned}S_i & = \partial \ln C / \partial \ln P_i \\ & = \beta_i + \beta_{iy} \ln y + \Sigma_m \beta_{im} \ln P_m + \Sigma_j \beta_{ij} \ln a_j + \beta_{Ti} T + \beta_{Tiy} T \ln y \\ & \quad + \Sigma_j \beta T_{ij} T \ln a_j + \Sigma_m \beta_{Tim} T \ln P_m + \beta_{Di} D + \varepsilon_i \qquad (3)\end{aligned}$$

In order for the cost function to be well-behaved, the restrictions of homogeneity of degree one in input prices, unity of sum of cost shares, and symmetry are imposed in the cost function and the cost-share equations. Since the set of equations has cross-equation restrictions, the optimal procedure is to jointly estimate the cost function and the cost share equations as a multivariate regression system. To avoid singularity, the cost share of purchased capital is excluded in the estimation process. To ensure invariance with respect to the choice of which share equation is dropped, the cost function and share equations of fuel, capital and labor are estimated jointly using the Full Information Maximum Likelihood technique.

4. DATA

The data used in this study consists of Class I and Class II common carriers which have an average of at least 75% of revenues from interstate traffic over the most recent three years and represent the LTL sector of the motor carrier industry. The data were collected annually by the American Trucking Association.[6] A panel data of 126 firms from 1976 to 1987 is constructed and there are 1,512 observations in the sample.

Firm output (y) is measured as total annual ton-miles. Total cost (C) is defined to include a 12% return to capital.[7] The vector of input prices consists of fuel (P_F), labor (P_L), purchased capital (P_R) and capital (P_K). The price of fuel is calculated as total fuel and oil expenses divided by an estimate of the number of gallons of fuel used. We assume that trucks average five miles per gallon and estimate gallons by dividing total vehicle miles by five. The price of labor is the firm's total employee compensation divided by the total number of employees. The price of purchased capital is total expenditures on purchased transportation divided by the total number of rented vehicle miles. The price of capital is calculated by dividing residual expenses (obtained by subtracting total fuel, labor, and purchased expenditures from total cost) by net operating property and equipment plus working capital.

In order to control for the heterogeneity between firms, four firm-specific attributes are incorporated in our models. These include average load (AL), average length of haul (ALH), average shipment size (AS) and insurance-per-tonmile (INS). AL describes the average weight of freight (measured in tons) and is defined as ton-miles divided by miles. Firms with higher AL will have lower unit costs. ALH captures the average distance traveled and is defined as ton-miles divided by tons. Firms serving longer distance are expected to have lower unit costs as total fixed cost, such as terminal expenses, are distributed over more units of output. AS captures the transaction and handling costs associated with shipments of different sizes (measured in tons) and is defined as total tons divided by total number of shipments. Firms with higher AS are expected to have lower unit costs due to the need for less handling and as smaller number of transactions. INS represents the average value of the commodities. As higher valued commodities require more insurance as well as additional services, unit costs will rise as INS increases. Total cost and input prices are deflated using factor price indices and expressed in 1988 constant dollars.

5. ESTIMATION RESULTS

A. Model Section

The first step in the analysis is to test for the existence of technological change and biases. To test whether a set of parameters associated with technological change and biases are significantly different from zero, a likelihood ratio test is used. The likelihood ratio statistic is defined as $-2\ (L_R - L_U)$, where L_R and L_U are the log of likelihood values of the restricted and unrestricted models, respectively. The statistic has a chi-square distribution with degrees of freedom equal to the number of parametric restrictions. Denoting equation (2) as the unrestricted model, the applicable likelihood ratio tests are:

1. No overall technology effect:

$$\beta_T = \beta_{TT} = \beta_{Ti} = \beta_{Tim} = \beta_{Ty} = \beta_{Tyy} = \beta_{Tiy} = \beta_{Tj} = \beta_{Tjn} = \beta_{Tij} = \beta_{Tjy} = \beta_{DT} = 0 \qquad (\forall i,m,j,n) \qquad (4)$$

2. No factor-input bias:

$$\beta_{Ti} = \beta_{Tim} = \beta_{Tiy} = \beta_{Tij} = 0 \qquad (\forall i,m,j,) \qquad (5)$$

3. No scale bias:

$$\beta_{Ty} = \beta_{Tyy} = \beta_{Tiy} = \beta_{Tjy} = 0 \qquad (\forall i,j,) \qquad (6)$$

4. No characteristic bias:

$$\beta_{Tj} = \beta_{Tij} = \beta_{Tjy} = \beta_{Tjn} = 0 \qquad (\forall i,j,n) \qquad (7)$$

5. No deregulation effect

$$\beta_D = \beta_{DT} = \beta_{Dy} = \beta_{Di} = \beta_{Dj} = 0 \qquad (\forall i,j,) \qquad (8)$$

Table 3 presents the estimated first order results from the full model (model 1) of Eq. (2), and the relevant restricted models. Restricted model 2 assumes no technological change or time effect. Given the presence of technological change, models 3 through 5 test the hypothesis of no input bias, scale bias, or attributes bias, respectively. Model 6 assumes no deregulation effect; models 7 and 8 test the hypothesis that deregulation has not altered the impact of attributes on costs and factor shares, respectively. Finally, model 9 assumes that the cost function could be represented as a second-order Taylor-series expansion in time and tests whether technology can be better explained by a third order approximation in time.

Table 3. Parameter Estimates: Full Model and Restricted Models.

Parameter	Full Model (Model 1)	Restricted Model 2	Restricted Model 3	Restricted Model 4	Restricted Model 5	Restricted Model 6	Restricted Model 7	Restricted Model 8	Restricted Model 9
ln y	1.0809	1.1184	1.0868	1.1095	1.1205	1.0713	1.0789	1.079	1.1301
	(19.44)	(50.02)	(21.45)	(46.80)	(43.09)	(19.73)	(19.41)	(19.48)	(44.58)
$(\ln y)^2$	−0.0017	0.0336	−0.0077	0.0337	0.0366	0.0003	−0.0023	−0.0017	0.0349
	(−0.07)	(4.05)	(−0.04)	(3.87)	(3.39)	(0.01)	(−0.10)	(−0.07)	(4.16)
$\ln P_F$	0.0609	0.0577	0.0577	0.0584	0.0607	0.0614	0.0608	0.0615	0.0589
	(15.48)	(35.87)	(34.85)	(19.76)	(29.64)	(16.37)	(15.70)	(16.11)	(30.41)
$\ln P_K$	0.2870	0.2913	0.2914	0.2916	0.2961	0.2849	0.2869	0.2850	0.2936
	(23.05)	(49.28)	(48.30)	(30.32)	(31.06)	(23.07)	(23.06)	(22.89)	(40.59)
$\ln P_L$	0.5767	0.5397	0.5499	0.5521	0.5675	0.5773	0.5763	0.5778	0.5548
	(33.15)	(67.99)	(66.64)	(40.81)	(48.67)	(34.23)	(33.54)	(33.61)	(56.35)
$\ln P_R$	0.0754	0.1113	0.1111	0.0980	0.0758	0.0763	0.0760	0.0757	0.0927
	(3.34)	(10.91)	(10.65)	(5.45)	(5.04)	(3.48)	(3.41)	(3.38)	(7.25)
ln AL	−0.3292	−0.5575	−0.3649	−0.2962	−0.5426	−0.3771	−0.3489	−0.3400	−0.5774
	(−2.14)	(−9.04)	(−2.49)	(−2.49)	(−8.69)	(−2.49)	(−2.24)	(−2.24)	(−7.50)
ln ALH	−0.4273	−0.5062	−0.4101	−0.5144	−0.5017	−0.3883	−0.3971	−0.4183	−0.5196
	(−3.72)	(−10.78)	(−3.94)	(−5.82)	(−10.47)	(−3.43)	(−3.45)	(−3.65)	(−9.31)
ln AS	−0.2520	−0.3096	−0.2583	−0.2868	−0.3102	−0.2487	−0.2364	−0.2512	−0.3046
	(−3.53)	(−10.36)	(−4.15)	(−5.39)	(−10.04)	(−3.54)	(−3.33)	(−3.52)	(−8.27)
ln INS	0.2456	0.1290	0.2666	0.2288	0.1134	0.2261	0.2650	0.2438	0.1223
	(1.79)	(2.37)	(2.10)	(2.09)	(2.00)	(1.64)	(1.90)	(1.78)	(1.75)
T	0.0540		0.0542	0.06307	0.0560	0.0633	0.0487	0.0593	0.04970
	(2.77)		(3.01)	(3.95)	(4.36)	(4.29)	(2.63)	(3.05)	(3.19)
T^2	−0.0139		−0.0140	−0.0141	−0.0127	−0.0064	−0.0131	−0.014	−0.01236
	(−4.58)		(−4.70)	(−4.68)	(−4.53)	(−5.10)	(−4.38)	(−4.60)	(−4.16)
T *ln y	0.0032		0.0026		−0.0019	0.0050	0.0054	0.0033	−0.0037
	(0.49)		(0.45)		(−0.72)	(0.82)	(0.84)	(0.50)	(−1.33)

Table 3. Continued

Parameter	Full Model (Model 1)	Restricted Model 2	Restricted Model 3	Restricted Model 4	Restricted Model 5	Restricted Model 6	Restricted Model 7	Restricted Model 8	Restricted Model 9
T *(ln y)^2	0.0053		0.0052		−0.0004	0.0049	0.0052	0.0053	
	(1.98)		(2.10)		(−0.44)	(1.89)	(1.95)	(1.98)	
T *ln P_F	−0.0006			−0.0002	−0.0006	−0.0010	−0.0006	−0.0010	−0.0003
	(−1.11)			(−0.58)	(−2.18)	(−2.34)	(−1.11)	(−2.34)	(−1.02)
T *ln P_K	0.0004			−0.0003	−0.0008	0.0018	0.0004	0.0017	−0.0005
	(0.24)			(−0.30)	(−0.67)	(1.26)	(0.25)	(1.22)	(−0.52)
T *ln P_L	−0.0069			−0.0033	−0.0056	−0.0076	−0.0068	−0.0076	−0.0034
	(−3.03)			(−1.90)	(−3.47)	(−3.78)	(−3.05)	(−3.69)	(−2.65)
T *ln P_R	0.0071			0.0039	0.0071	0.0068	0.0070	0.0068	0.0041
	(2.50)			(1.75)	(3.70)	(2.64)	(2.51)	(2.63)	(2.56)
T *ln AL	−0.0250		−0.0200	−0.0292		−0.0169	−0.0177	−0.0238	0.0051
	(−1.37)		(−1.17)	(−2.19)		(−0.98)	(−1.00)	(−1.32)	(0.60)
T *ln ALH	−0.0088		−0.0114	0.0014		−0.020	−0.0184	−0.0105	0.0053
	(−0.59)		(−0.87)	(0.14)		(−1.54)	(−1.37)	(−0.71)	(0.69)
T *ln AS	−0.0083		−0.0068	−0.0037		−0.015	−0.0142	−0.0090	0.0001
	(−1.05)		(−0.98)	(−0.70)		(−2.00)	(−1.87)	(−1.15)	(0.03)
T *ln INS	−0.0135		−0.016	−0.0124		−0.0145	−0.0140	−0.01475	0.0003
	(−0.88)		(−1.13)	(−1.09)		(−0.98)	(−0.94)	(−0.97)	(0.04)
D	−0.2059	0.1862	−0.2234	−0.2499	−0.1679		−0.1851	−0.2553	−0.1574
	(−1.74)	(4.96)	(−1.94)	(−2.15)	(−1.64)		(−1.81)	(−2.18)	(−1.35)
D *T	0.0665		0.0687	0.06691	0.0574		0.0638	0.0663	0.0585
	(3.32)		(3.52)	(3.34)	(2.98)		(3.17)	(3.32)	(2.98)
D *ln P_F	−0.0046	−0.0063	−0.0063	−0.0046	−0.0042		−0.0046		−0.0047
	(−2.17)	−(5.29)	(−5.14)	(−2.18)	(−2.16)		(−2.36)		(−2.28)
D *ln P_K	0.0139	0.0118	0.0111	0.0141	0.0138		0.0140		0.0138
	(1.94)	(2.78)	(2.56)	(1.98)	(2.06)		(2.07)		(2.02)

Table 3. Continued.

Parameter	Full Model (Model 1)	Restricted Model 2	Restricted Model 3	Restricted Model 4	Restricted Model 5	Restricted Model 6	Restricted Model 7	Restricted Model 8	Restricted Model 9
D *ln P_L	−0.0061	−0.0274	−0.0274	−0.0063	−0.0068		0.0064		−0.0078
	(−0.65)	(−4.74)	(−4.53)	(−0.66)	(−0.75)		(−0.70)		(−0.87)
D *ln P_R	−0.0032	−0.2187	0.0226	−0.0032	−0.0029		−0.0031		−0.0014
	(−0.26)	(−2.94)	(2.88)	(−0.27)	(−0.26)		(−0.26)		(−0.12)
D *ln AL	0.0589	0.1071	0.0557	0.0700	0.1181			0.0560	0.0892
	(0.93)	(2.73)	(0.91)	(1.13)	(3.05)			(0.89)	(1.49)
D *ln ALH	−0.0732	−0.0235	−0.0694	−0.0363	−0.0347			−0.0710	−0.0656
	(−1.21)	(−0.7377)	(−1.20)	(−0.67)	(−1.07)			(−1.22)	(−1.13)
D *ln AS	−0.0511	−0.0432	−0.0500	−0.0505	−0.0418			−0.0505	−0.0429
	(−1.61)	(−2.45)	(−1.66)	(−1.59)	(−2.28)			(−1.66)	(−1.43)
D *ln INS	0.0176	0.0258	0.0174	0.0058	0.0491			0.0195	0.0402
	(0.30)	(0.76)	(0.31)	(0.0980)	(1.39)			(0.33)	(0.73)
D *ln y	0.0179	−0.0131	0.0168	−0.0066	0.0021		−0.0039		0.0152
	(0.75)	(−0.95)	(0.74)	(−0.44)	(0.12)		(−0.28)		(0.68)
Log likelihood	8,499.51	8,423.18	8,468.09	8486.61	8,466.09	8,474.96	8,495.42	8,490.38	8,452.81

t-statistics in parenthesis

As shown, all the first order estimates of output, input prices, and attributes have the expected signs and are highly significant. The coefficients of output are greater than one for all models, implying that the representative firm exhibits mild diseconomies of scale. The negative signs of AL, ALH, and AS indicate that the representative firm can achieve lower costs by increasing these network attributes. The positive coefficient on INS shows that higher costs are associated with higher value shipments, a result that makes intuitive sense since extra service and handling costs may be required.

All the time trend coefficients (β_T) are positive, indicating that costs have risen over time. All of the second order coefficients (β_{TT}) are negative. Since the time trend is treated as a technology variable, these results indicate that the trucking industry has experienced a decrease in productivity over time, but that the rate of productivity decline is rapidly decreasing. Based on the magnitude of β_{TT}, the pure impact of technological change appears to be cost saving.

The coefficient for the first order deregulation variable is negative in all models and significant, except in model 2. This indicates that the direct impact of deregulation was to shift the cost function downward. However, all of the estimates of the interaction terms between deregulation and time are positive and significant, suggesting that deregulation has increased costs through a negative impact on technological change. As argued by McMullen & Okuyama (2000), this technological regress may reflect the deregulation-induced adjustments made in firm's operations as a result of regulatory changes.

Since model 2 does not assume any technology effect, the positive value of β_D only reflects the net negative effect of deregulation on productivity over the sample period. Including the time trend, the deregulation dummy, and their interactions in the cost function allows us to separate the impacts of technology and deregulation on productivity. For example, based on the interactions between D and input prices, model 2 indicates that deregulation has reduced the cost shares of fuel, labor and purchased capital, but raised the share of capital. Moreover, these changes are shown to be statistically significant. However, with both the time trend and deregulation included in the full model (model 1), results suggest that only the increase in capital share and the decrease in fuel share are attributed to the impact of deregulation; the reduction of the labor cost share and the increase in the cost share of purchased capital are caused by exogenous technological change. Therefore, modeling the cost function without the time trend would lead to omitted variable bias.

Table 4 presents the results of the likelihood ratio tests described above. Based on the Chi-square statistics, we can reject all of the restricted models except model 7. Therefore, we accept the hypothesis that technological change

Table 4. Likelihood Ratio Test.

Model	$-2\ (L_R - L_U)$	Restrictions	Significance
2 (No Technology Effect)	152.70	57	0.005
3 (No Input Bias)	62.84	32	0.005
4 (No Scale Bias)	25.80	10	0.005
5 (No Attribute Bias)	66.84	34	0.005
6 (No Deregulation Effect)	49.10	11	0.005
7 (Deregulation does not affect firm's attributes)	8.18	4	Not significance
8 (Deregulation does not affect input shares)	18.26	4	0.005
9 (2nd order expansion in T)	93.40	41	0.005

Notes: Full Model is the unrestricted model (L_U). Model 1–8 are the restricted models (L_R).

Table 5. Chow Test.

	1976–1979	1980–1987	1976–1987
Sum of squares residuals	21.02	51.29	74.75
Sample size	$N_1 = 504$	$N_2 = 1008$	$N_1 + N_2 = 1512$
Number of parameters: 117			

in the trucking industry has induced bias toward input, output, and attributes. In addition, the likelihood ratio tests show that, although deregulation has had an impact on productivity growth and factor shares, it has not altered the relationship between attributes and costs of the representative firm.

The last step in the model selection concerns the stability of parameters over time. Since the sample data span the 1976 to 1987 period, we conducted a Chow Test to test whether the parameters in the cost function were stable over the pre- and post- deregulation period. Dividing the sample into pre- and post-deregulation periods, we estimated three translog cost functions based on model 7 and obtained the following sum of squares residuals:

The F statistic for testing the restriction that all the coefficients pre- and post-deregulation cost functions are the same is 0.37. Since the critical value is 1.48 at 1% significance level, we could not reject the hypothesis that the coefficient vectors are the same in the two periods. Therefore, we can evaluate the technological change and any associated bias based on the results from model 7.

B. Technological Change

Productivity growth and technological change can be measured by differentiating the cost function with respect to time to obtain the following expression:

$$\partial \ln C/\partial T = \beta_T + \beta_{TT}\, T + \Sigma_i \beta_{Ti} \ln P_i + \Sigma_j \beta_{Tj} \ln a_j + \beta_{Ty} \ln y + {}^1\!/_2\, \beta_{Tyy} (\ln y)^2$$
$$+ {}^1\!/_2\, \Sigma_i \Sigma_m \beta_{Tim} \ln P_i \ln P_m + \Sigma_i \beta_{Tiy} \ln P_i \ln y + \Sigma_i \Sigma_j \beta_{Tij} \ln P_i \ln a_j$$
$$+ \Sigma_j \beta_{Tjy} \ln a_j \ln y + {}^1\!/_2\, \Sigma_j \Sigma_n \beta_{Tjn} \ln a_j \ln a_n + \beta_{DT} D \qquad (9)$$

By evaluating the above expression at the sample mean for output, input prices, and firms' attributes, we can estimate the percentage change in costs for the "representative" firm due to technological advancement or decline over the sample period:

$$\partial \ln C/\partial T = \beta_T + \beta_{TT} T + \beta_{DT} D \qquad (10)$$

As indicated in Eq. (10), the percentage change in cost over time consists of two components: (1) the effect of exogenous technological change as captured by $\beta_T + \beta_{TT} T$, where the estimate of β_T captures the pure technological impact on the representative firm's costs over time while the second-order estimate, β_{TT}, captures its rate of change, and (2) the effect of deregulation on technological change as captured by $\beta_{DT} D$, where β_{DT} is the estimate of the interaction between the time trend and the deregulation variable. The overall impact of technological change on cost depends on the sum of these two effects.

The results from model 7 show that the estimates of β_T and β_{TT} are 0.0487 and −0.0131 respectively. Both of the parameter estimates are significant at 1% level. Without the impact of the deregulation, we would expect the total cost of the representative firm to change by $\beta_T + \beta_{TT} T$ at the end of year T; at the expansion point, the pure productivity effect ($\partial \ln C/\partial T = \beta_T + \beta_{TT} T$ for $T = 12$) would have reduced cost by an average of 10.85% over the sample period. The estimate of β_{DT} is 0.0638 with a t-statistic of 3.17. Therefore, deregulation has reduced the rate of productivity growth by 6.38%. Overall, the results suggest that productivity growth has caused a 4.47% decrease in cost for the representative firm over the sample period.

C. Input Bias and Factor Substitutability

The input bias can be obtained by differentiating equation (9) with respect to each of the input prices:

$$I_{bi} = \partial^2 \ln C/\partial T \, \partial \ln P_i$$
$$= \beta_{Ti} + \Sigma_m \beta_{Tim} \ln P_m + \beta_{Tiy} \ln y + \Sigma_j \beta_{Tij} \ln a_j \qquad (11)$$

According to the Young's theorem, $\partial^2 \ln C/\partial T \, \partial \ln P_i = \partial^2 \ln C/\partial \ln P_i \, \partial T$. The input bias, I_{bi}, thus measures the change in input share with respect to time. A positive I_{bi} implies that technological change is relatively ith factor using, while a negative I_{bi} implies a relative ith factor saving and $I_i = 0$ implies neutrality. Table 6 shows the second-order and selected third-order estimates for measuring input bias.

The coefficients β_{Ti} capture the impact of technological change on the ith factor's share for the representative firm operating at the sample mean. Therefore, the estimate of β_{TL} and β_{TR} suggest that technological change has reduced the labor's cost share by 0.68% per year and increased purchased capital's share by 0.7% per year. Judging from the t-statistics for β_{TF} and β_{TK}, the cost shares of fuel and capital have not been affected by technological change. This implies that technology change has caused the representative firm to become more purchased-capital intensive and less labor intensive over time, but has not altered the intensity of fuel and capital. These results suggest that some of the job loss in the LTL sector is attributable to technological change.

The source of input bias can be examined by taking additional derivatives of Eq. (11) with respect to input price, output, and firm's attributes. According to Binswanger (1974a, b), changes in relative input prices can have a strong impact on the direction of technological change. For example, changes in the wage rate could encourage producers to focus on labor-saving research which would lead to labor-saving technological bias. Therefore, the coefficients β_{Tim}

Table 6. Parameter Estimates for Input Bias.

Parameter	Estimate	Parameter	Estimate	Parameter	Estimate
β_{TF}	−0.0006 (−1.11)	β_{TFY}	−0.0002 (−1.34)	β_{TFF}	−0.0002 (−0.71)
β_{TK}	0.0004 (0.25)	β_{TKY}	0.0004 (0.74)	β_{TKK}	−0.0003 (−0.97)
β_{TL}	−0.0068** (−3.05)	β_{TLY}	−0.0020** (−3.09)	β_{TLL}	0.0009 (0.50)
β_{TR}	0.0070** (2.51)	β_{TRY}	0.0018** (2.29)	β_{TRR}	0.002 (0.70)

t-statistics in parenthesis.
** Indicates significant at the 0.01 level.

in Eq. (11) capture the extent to which input bias is induced by changes in input prices. According to the estimates reported in table 6, all the estimates of β_{Tim} are small and insignificant. Therefore, the labor and purchased capital shares biases are not driven by changes in input prices.

Similarly, an increase in the scale of output will tend to increase research effort and affect the direction of technological change. The coefficients β_{Tiy} capture the impact of output changes on input bias. Based on the third-order estimates of β_{TLY} and β_{TRY}, the labor and purchased-capital shares biases appear to be output-augmented, i.e. the cost share bias of labor and purchased capital vary with respect to the output level. Firms whose output are beyond the expansion point by 1% would experience a further reduction of labor cost share of 0.2% and an additional increase in the purchased capital share of 0.18%.

In addition to analyzing the input bias, we can investigate whether technological change has altered the substitutability between inputs over time. For the representative firm operating at mean level of output, input prices, and attributes, the elasticities of substitution are given by:

$$\sigma_{im} = (\beta_{im} + S_i S_m + \beta_{Tim}\,T)/S_i S_m \qquad i \neq m \tag{12}$$

$$\sigma_{ii} = (\beta_{ii} + S_i\,(S_i - 1) + \beta_{Tii}\,T)/S_i \tag{13}$$

where S_i and S_m are the fitted shares of the ith and the mth inputs. The own-price and cross-price elasticities are reported in table 7.

As shown in Table 7, all the own-price elasticities of demand have the correct signs, with purchased capital exhibiting the highest, and fuel having the lowest, elasticity of demand. As observed by Friedlaender and Bruce (1985), these figures reflect the fact that purchased capital is often treated as a residual input by LTL trucking firms to carry peak loads, while fuel is an essential input for the line-haul journey.

Consistent with results of previous studies, the elasticities of substitution indicate that all four inputs are substitutes for one another. As expected, capital

Table 7. Elasticities of Substitution (Evaluated at the Sample Mean).

	Fuel	Capital	Labor	Purchased Capital
Fuel	−0.3053	0.5517	1.1200	0.8931
Capital		−0.6750	0.9868	1.7811
Labor			−0.3518	1.2260
Purchased Capital				−0.7995

and purchased-capital appear to be highly substitutable; as the cost of owned capital goes up, firms will find it more beneficial to employ outside resources. Since purchased-capital often includes labor and fuel, its substitutability between labor and fuel are also noticeably high. The relatively high substitution between fuel and labor appears to be counter-intuitive as one would expect these two inputs to be complements of each other. However, the increase in LTL operations also result in an increase in terminal operations which are very labor intensive relative to line-haul operations. In addition, the adoption of information systems has resulted in a reduction in delivery time and distance traveled. Therefore, the substitution between fuel and labor may reflect the changing production process. This line of reasoning is consistent with the impact of technological change on the elasticity of substitution between fuel and labor shown in Table 7. The positive time-derivative indicates that fuel and labor became more substitutable over time.

To see whether technological change has altered the substitutability between inputs over time, we take the derivative of the elasticity of substitution with respect to time:

$$\partial \sigma_{im} / \partial T = [(\beta_{Tim} S_i S_m - (\beta_{im} + \beta_{Tim} T)(\beta_{Tm} S_i + \beta_{Ti} S_m)]/(S_i S_m)^2 \quad i \neq m \quad (14)$$

$$\partial \sigma_{ii} / \partial T = [(\beta_{Tii} S_i - \beta_{Ti} (\beta_{ii} + \beta_{Tii} T) + \beta_{Ti} S_i^2)]/S_i^2 \quad (15)$$

The results are reported in Table 8.

Based on the derivatives of own-price elasticities with respect to time, technological change appears to have reduced the price elasticities of fuel, capital, and purchased capital, but increased the price elasticity of labor.[8] These results suggest that employment in the trucking industry may have become more sensitive to changes in labor market conditions. With the exception of fuel and labor, all the other time-derivatives for input substitutions are negative, and rather

Table 8. Mean Derivatives of Elasticities of Substitution with Respect to Time (Evaluated at the Sample Mean).

	Fuel	Capital	Labor	Purchased Capital
Fuel	0.0105	−0.0077	0.0126	−0.0937
Capital		0.0032	−0.0002	−0.0071
Labor			−0.0035	−0.0023
Purchased Capital				0.0200

small, suggesting that technological change has generally reduced the elasticity of substitution between inputs.[9] In fact, technological development may have changed the role of individual inputs. For example, a firm's own capital may be used primarily toward expanding network facilities and terminal operations which may not be easily substituted for purchased capital; therefore, the time-derivative of the substitution between capital and purchased capital is negative. Similarly, purchased-capital has become less substitutable with labor and fuel over time. This indicates that the traditional residual role of purchased capital may have changed over time.

D. Economies of Scale and Output Bias

Economies of scale (S_c) in the dual cost function can be calculated by $\partial \ln C/\partial \ln y$ and is given by the following expression.

$$S_c = \partial \ln C/\partial \ln y = \beta_y + \beta_{yy} \ln y + \Sigma_i \beta_{iy} \ln P_i + \Sigma_j \beta_{jy} \ln a_j$$
$$+ \beta_{Ty} T + \beta_{Tyy} T \ln y + \Sigma_i \beta_{Tiy} T \ln P_i + \Sigma_j \beta_{Tjy} T \ln a_j + \beta_{Dy} D \tag{16}$$

From the cost function perspective, S_c less than 1 implies the existence of economies of scale, S_c equal to 1 implies constant returns to scale, and Sc greater than 1 implies diseconomies of scale. Table 9 presents the estimates that are needed to calculate the economies of scale based on Eq. (16).

The estimate of β_y is 1.0798 with a t-statistic of 19.4, implying mildly decreasing returns to scale. The coefficient β_{YY} reflects whether or not economies of scale depends on the level of output. The negative value of β_{YY} indicates that scale economies can be achieved at higher levels of output; however, it is not statistically significant. Moreover, economies of scale are not affected by the operating attributes since all the interaction terms between output and firm's attributes are insignificant. Therefore, even if regulatory policies affected firms' attributes, they would not have any indirect effect on technological advancement. However, scale economies could change as the representative firm alters its input mix in response to changes in input prices and output level. The negative sign for β_{RY} indicates that scale economies increase with higher purchased capital price. Note that the coefficients for the interaction between input prices and output also shows how cost shares change in response to changes in output level. This implies that scale economies are affected by substitution between inputs as well as the output levels. Similarly, the positive sign of β_{LY} implies that economies of scale would decrease with a higher labor price. This is probably due to the inability to substitute other inputs for labor as firms expand their output level.

Table 9. Parameter Estimates for Economies of Scale.

Parameter	Estimate	Parameter	Estimate
β_{Y}	1.0798** (19.41)	β_{TY}	0.0054 (0.84)
β_{YY}	−0.0022 (−0.10)	β_{TYY}	0.0052** (1.95)
β_{FY}	−0.0010 (−0.88)	β_{TFY}	−0.0002 (−1.33)
β_{KY}	−0.0063 (−1.47)	β_{TKY}	0.0004 (0.28)
β_{LY}	0.0251** (5.07)	β_{TLY}	−0.0019** (−3.09)
β_{RY}	−0.0178** (−2.99)	β_{TRY}	0.0018** (2.29)
β_{ALY}	−0.0381 (−0.74)	β_{TALY}	0.0004 (0.06)
β_{ALHY}	0.0533 (1.18)	β_{TALHY}	−0.0072 (−1.42)
β_{ASY}	0.0110 (0.45)	β_{TASY}	−0.0028 (−0.67)
β_{INSY}	0.0232 (0.62)	β_{TINSY}	0.0024 (0.57)

t-statistics in parenthesis.

** Indicates significant at the 0.01 level.

Output bias can be obtained by differentiating Eq. (16) with respect to time as follows:

$$O_b = \partial^2 \ln C/\partial T \, \partial \ln y = \beta_{Ty} + \beta_{Tyy} \ln y + \Sigma_i \beta_{Tiy} \ln P_i + \Sigma_j \beta_{Tjy} \ln a_j \quad (17)$$

The output bias, O_b, measures the impact of technological change on returns-to-scale for the dual production function over time. Such a bias would alter the range over which returns to scale of a given degree could be realized and thus alter the output level at which minimum average costs could be attained. For example, if economies of scale increase over time (i.e. $O_b < 0$ implies, over time, cost declines as output increases), the minimum efficient scale (MES)[10]would increase and the number of firms in the industry would decline over time, leading to a rise in concentration ratio. Similarly, O_b greater than 0 implies MES is decreasing and the concentration ratio in the industry would fall over time. Finally, O_i equals to 0 implies no change in MES. Therefore, a scale-biased technological change would alter the minimum scale required for efficient firm operation and thus have significant antitrust policy implications. Since O_b is also a function of output, we can test the Schumpeter hypothesis that large firms have a more rapid rate of technological advancement than small firms. If the Schumpeter hypothesis holds, we would expect $\partial \ln C/\partial T$ decreases with output so that O_b is less than zero. At the expansion point, this would be the case if the sign of β_{Ty} is negative.

The output bias of technological change on the representative firm is captured by the estimate of β_{Ty}. As indicated in Table 9, the estimate of β_{Ty} is not significantly different from zero, implying that returns to scale have not changed over time. Since $\beta_{Ty} > 0$, the results do not support the Schumpeter hypothesis in the trucking industry. The estimate of β_{TiY} shows whether changes in scale economies are induced by changes in input prices. Based on the signs of β_{TLY} and β_{TRY}, an increase in the price of labor and a decrease in price of purchased capital are associated with an increase in scale economies. All the third-order estimates of the interactions between the time trend, output, and firm's attributes are not significant. Therefore, firm' attributes have not affected economies of scale over time.

E. Characteristics Bias

The characteristic bias, A_{bj}, measures the relationship between technological change and the firm's attributes, and can be obtained by differentiating Eq. (9) with respect to each of the firm's attributes:

$$A_{bj} = \partial^2 \ln C/\partial T\, \partial \ln a_j = \beta_{Tj} + \Sigma_i \beta_{Tij} \ln P_i + \beta_{Tjy} \ln y + \Sigma_n \beta_{Tjn} \ln a_n \quad (18)$$

Since attributes may capture qualitative aspects of each firm's network, we would expect the impact of characteristics on costs to change as firms expand their use of information technology. As the firm's network increases, we would expect the firm's participation in LTL traffic to increase, possibly offering more frequent service. Therefore, we expect the sign of $\beta_{T,AS}$ and $\beta_{T,AL}$ to be negative reflecting an increase in cost savings associated with larger shipment size and load over time. Also, as firms adopt computerized routing systems, freight should follow a more direct path between two points rather than making unnecessary trips. Since the average length of haul captures the distance traveled per ton, we expect the sign of $\beta_{T,ALH}$ to be negative reflecting an increase in cost savings from longer haul. The insurance variable serves as a proxy for the fragility and value of the commodities carried by the firm. Because fragile, valuable commodities tend to require special handling, cost should be positively related to this variable. But as technology reduces time in route, dock, and load planning, handling cost should be lowered. Therefore, we would expect the

Table 10. Parameter Estimates for Characteristics Bias.

Parameter	Estimate	Parameter	Estimate
β_{TAL}	−0.0177	β_{TALH}	−0.0184
	(−1.00)		(−1.37)
β_{TAS}	−0.0142*	β_{TINS}	−0.0140
	(−1.87)		(−0.94)
t-statistics in parenthesis.			

* Indicates significant at the 0.10 level.

impact of insurance per ton-mile to decrease over time. Since previous regulatory policies, such as commodity and route restrictions, directly affected firms' characteristics, the estimated characteristics bias may reveal the indirect effect of deregulation on technical change through firms' characteristics.

Table 10 shows the first-order estimates of the interactions between the time trend and the firm's attributes. As expected, all the interaction terms between time and the firm's attributes are negative; however, only the estimate of β_{TAS} is significant at 10% level. As firms expand their LTL traffic and offer more frequent service, the cost savings associated with larger shipment size has increased over time. It appears that technological change has not significantly altered the impact of firm's attributes on costs over time.

F. Impact of Deregulation

Following Ying (1990b), the effect of deregulation on trucking technology can be measured by calculating the percentage change in cost due to a unit change in the deregulation variable:

$$\frac{(C_1 - C_0)}{C_0} \bullet 100 = \left[\exp\left(\beta_D + \beta_{DT} T + \sum_i \beta_{Di} \ln P_i + \beta_{Dy} \ln y \right) - 1 \right] \bullet 100 \qquad (19)$$

Table 11 presents the estimates that are needed to calculate the effect of deregulation on costs.

At the expansion point, the estimate of β_D captures the direct impact of deregulation on the representative firm's cost structure and the estimate of β_{DT} captures the direct impact of deregulation on technology change as discussed earlier. The estimate of β_D is −0.1851 with a t-statistics of −1.81. Therefore,

Table 11. Parameter Estimates for Deregulation Impact.

Parameter	Estimate	Parameter	Estimate
β_D	−0.1851* (−1.81)	β_{DF}	−0.0046** (−2.36)
β_{DT}	0.0638** (3.17)	β_{DK}	0.0140** (2.07)
β_{DY}	−0.0039 (−0.28)	β_{DL}	−0.0064 (−0.70)
		β_{DR}	−0.0031 (−0.26)

t-statistics in parenthesis.

* Indicates significant at the 0.05 level.
** Indicates significant at the 0.01 level.

the direct impact of deregulation was to reduce cost by 16.9% over the sample period. However, the positive sign of β_{DT} indicates that deregulation has caused costs to rise over time. Evaluated at the expansion point, deregulation has caused the total cost of a representative firm to increase by 78.7%.[11] This result is inconsistent with the findings of Ying (1990b) whose simulation, based on the sample mean for each year, shows cost savings of 22.84% by 1984. We consider our estimate of the direct impact of deregulation as reasonable and consistent with the general results of previous studies. The difference being the deregulation-induced productivity decline which is similar to the results of McMullen and Okuyama (2000). The cost increase captured by the interaction of the time trend with deregulation could also reflect the change in service mix and quality after deregulation. For example, cost per ton-mile may increase over time if firms now offer very rapid delivery, more reliability, frequent, and convenient services.

The estimates of the interaction terms between D and the input prices (P_i) and output capture the direct impact of deregulation on the cost shares and economies of scale, respectively. For example, a negative value for β_{Di} indicates that deregulation has been ith input saving, while a positive value for β_{Di} indicates that deregulation has been *i*th input using. Therefore, the estimates of β_{DF} and β_{DK} suggest that deregulation has reduced the cost share of fuel by 0.46% and increased the cost share of capital by 1.4%. The estimate of β_{DY} is not statistically significant, indicating that deregulation did not alter scale economies in the trucking industry.

6. CONCLUSION

Using the approach developed by Stevenson (1980), we have analyzed technological bias and the impact of deregulation on the cost structure of the LTL sector of the motor carrier industry. Other things held constant, deregulation has caused the representative firm to use less fuel and more capital. The reduction in fuel cost share may reflect efficiency gains due to the elimination of route restrictions. The increase in capital cost share may correspond to the growth in terminals and network capacity after deregulation. For example, Arkansas-Best Freight System, Inc. (ABF) finds that, in order to compete in the post-deregulation environment, it is necessary to expand the scope of coverage and services, and as a result, it has increased the number of terminal facilities by over 550% between 1976 and 1995.

Although its direct impact was favorable, deregulation has reduced productivity and led to higher industry costs. As indicated in the section on model selection, this deregulation-induced productivity decline is robust across all tested models, though it should be interpreted with caution. First, deregulation coincided with recession; second, firms expanded their scope of services since deregulation. Therefore, the increase in cost over time, as indicated by the interaction between time trend and the deregulation variable, may have been caused by poor adjustments or differences in service quality. Without further data at the micro level to control for service mix and other relevant factors, such as number of terminals and network layouts, the actual cause of "productivity decline" is difficult to decompose.

Our results show that technological bias is present in the twelve-year sample period. Technological change has been relatively labor saving, and purchased-capital using. These input biases were not driven by changes in input prices, but were induced by output level. Therefore, the expansion path of the representative firm is not linear. As output increases, cost minimization requires a reduction in labor's cost share and an increase in the share of purchased capital. Technological change has increased the economies of larger shipment size over time, but has not significantly altered the impact of average load, average length of haul, or insurance per tonmile on costs over time. The output bias of technological change on the representative firm is not significant and our results do not support the Schumpeter hypothesis in the LTL sector of the motor carrier industry.

Over time, the LTL sector of the motor carrier industry has become relatively less labor and fuel intensive and more capital (both own and rental) intensive. Firms continue to expand their terminal networks and utilize new technology such as computerized management information systems for route and service expansion. All this requires substantial capital investment resulting in even higher entry barriers. The largest and financially strongest carriers, such as Yellow Freight System, Consolidated Frightways and Roadway Express, have become much more dominant than ever. Although the observed increase in industry concentration can be partially explained by the presence of input bias, it cannot be soundly justified because of the absence of scale economies.

NOTES

1. Breen (1982).
2. Harmatuck (1990).
3. *Trucking Regulation: Price Competition and Market Structure in the Trucking Industry*, U.S. General Accounting Office, February 1987, p. 16.
4. The HHI approaches zero under perfect competition and takes on a value of 10000 under monopoly. The U.S. Department of Justice Merger guidelines consider markets with an HHI below 1000 to be unconcentrated, those with an HHI between 1000 and 1800 as moderately concentrated and those with an HHI greater than 1800 as highly concentrated.
5. By ICC classification there are large (Class I), medium-size (Class II) and small (Class III) common carriers. Instruction 27 carriers are Class I and II motor carriers (i.e. those with annual revenues of more than $1 million) that have an average of at least 75% of revenues from interstate traffic over the most recent three years. According to the American Trucking Association, LTL carriers generally fall into this category.
6. We would like to thank Professor Tom Corsi for providing the ATA data tapes.
7. C = TOE + 0.12*(NOPE + WC) where TOE is total operating expenses, NOPE is net operating property and equipment, and WC is net current assets, or working capital.
8. Since the sign of own price elasticity of demand is always negative, a negative time-derivative indicates an increase in price elasticity while a positive time-derivative indicates an decrease in price elasticity.
9. As indicated in Table 8, two inputs are substitutes if their cross-price elasticity is positive; other things held constant, firm can substitute input i for input j in response to an increase in price of input *j*. Therefore, if the time derivative of the elasticity of substitution is negative, the two inputs become less substitutable of each other over time.
10. The MES is defined as the output level at which average cost is at its minimum.
11. We also try to perform the same simulations as suggested by Ying (1990b), but problems arise. This is not uncommon when flexible functional forms are used to make predictions at points away from the sample mean. Winston et al. (1990) also experienced similar difficulties when they tried to predict deregulated costs for individual carriers and railroads. Therefore, our analysis focuses on the impact of the representative firms as evaluated at the sample mean. Terrence J. Wales, On the Flexibility of Flexible Functional Forms: An Empirical Approach. *Journal of Econometrics*, *5*(March 1977), 183–193, provides a general discussion of this problem.

REFERENCES

Allen, W. B. (1990). Deregulation and Information. *Transportation Journal* (Winter), 58–67.

Allen, W. B., & Liu, D. (1985). Service quality and motor carrier costs: An empirical analysis. *The Review of Economics and Statistics*, Vol LXXVII, *3* (August), 499–509.

Adrangi, B., Chow, G., & Raffiee, K. (1995). Analysis of the Deregulation of the U.S. Trucking Industry. *Journal of Transportation Economics and Policy* (September), 233–246.

Averch, H., & Johnson, L. L. (1962). Behavior of the Firm under Regulatory Constraint. *American Economic Review*, 52 (December): 1052–1069.

Blackorby, C., Knox Lovell, C. A., & Thursby, M. C. (1976). Extended Hicks Neutral Technical Change. *The Economic Journal, 86* (December), 845–852.

Binswanger, H. P. (1974a). The Measurement of Technical Change Biases with Many Factors of Production. *American Economic Review, 64* (December), 964–976.

Binswanger, H. P. (1974b). A Microeconomic Approach to Induced Innovation. *Economic Journal, 84* (December), 940–958.

Booa, A., & Hamilton. (1982). Impact on Transportation Management Changes in the Collective Ratemaking System. Washington, D.C. Report for the Motor Common Carrier Association (July).

Boyer, K. D. (1993). Deregulation of the Trucking Sector: Specialization, Concentration, Entry, and Financial Distress. *Southern Economic Journal* (January), 485–495.

Breen, D. A. (1982). Regulatory Reform and the Trucking Industry: An Evaluation of the Motor Carrier Act of 1980. Report submitted to Motor Carrier Ratemaking Study Commission, Bureau of Economics, Federal Trade Commission (March).

Brunning, E. R. (1992). Cost Efficiency Measurement in the Trucking Industry: An Application of the Stochastic Frontier Approach. *International Journal of Transport Economics*, Vol. xix, *2* (June), 165–186.

Chiang, W., & Friedlaender, A. F. (1984). Output Aggregation, Network Effects, and the Measurement of Trucking Technology. *Review of Economics and Statistics*, *66*(2), 267–276.

Chiang, W., & Friedlaender, A. F. (1985). Truck Technology and Efficient Market Structure. *Review of Economics and Statistics*, *67*(2), 250–258.

Capron, W. M. (1971). *Technological Change in Regulated Industries: Studies in the Regulation of Economic Activity*. Washington, D.C.: The Brookings Institution.

Consolidated Freightways Inc. (1995). Annual Report to Shareholders.

Corsi, T., Grimm, C. M., & Feitler, J. (1992). The impact of Deregulation on LTL Motor Carriers: Size, Structure, and Organization. *Transportation Journal* (Winter), 24–31.

Daniel, T. P., & Kleit, A. N. (1995). Disentangling Regulatory Policy: The Effects of State Regulations on Trucking Rates. Bureau of Economics Staff Report. Federal Trade Commission (November).

Fare, R., Grosskopf, S., & Lee, W. F. (1995). Productivity and Technical Change. Southern Illinois University at Carbondale, working paper #95-16.

Fellner, W. (1961). Two Propositions in the Theory of Induced Innovations. *Economic Journal, 71* (June), 305–308.

Friedlaender, A. F., & Bruce, S. S. (1985). Augmentation Effects and Technical Change in the Regulated Trucking Industry, 1974–1979. In: A. F. Daughety (Ed.), *Analytical Studies in Transport Economics*. Cambridge: Cambridge University Press.

Galbraith, J. K. (1952). *American Capitalism.* Boston: Houghton Mifflin Company.

Glaskowsky, N. A. Jr. (1990). *Effect of Deregulation on Motor Carriers* (2nd ed.). Connecticut: The Eno Foundation for Transportation.

Harmatuck, J. D. (1990). Motor Carrier Cost Function Comparison. *Transportation Journal* (Summer), 31–46.

Hausman, J. A. (1983). Information Costs, Competiton, and Collective Ratemaking in the Motor Carrier Industry. *The American University Law Review*, *32*, 377–392.

Hicks, J. R. (1932). *The Theory of Wages*. London: Macmillan & Co. Ltd.

Keeler, T. E. (1986). Public Policy and Productivity in the Trucking Industry: Some Evidence on the Effects of Highway Investments, Deregulation, and the 55 MPH Speed Limit. *American Economic Review, Papers and Proceedings*, *76*(2) (May), 153–158.

Kling, R. W. (1990). Deregulation and Structural Change in the LTL Motor Freight Industry. *Transportation Journal* (Spring), 47–53.

Mcmullen, B. S. (1987). The Impact of Regulatory Reform on U.S. Motor Carrier Costs. *Journal of Transport Economics and Policy* (September), 307–319.

McMullen, B. S., & Stanley, L.R. (1988). The Impact of Deregulation on the Production Structure of the Motor Carrier Industry. *Economic Inquiry*, *26*, 299–316.

McMullen, B. S., & Tanaka, H. (1995). An Econometric Analysis of Differences Between Motor Carriers: Implications for Market Structure, *Quarterly Journal of Business and Economics*, *34*, 3–16.

McMullen, B. S., & Okuyama, K. (2000). Productivity Changes in the U.S. Motor Carrier Industry Following Deregulation: A Malmquist Index Approach. *International Journal of Transport Economics* (forthcoming).

McMullen, B. S., & Lee, M.-K. (1999). Cost Efficiency in the U.S. Motor Carrier Industry Before and After Deregulation: A Stochastic Frontier Approach. *Journal of Transport Economics and Policy*, *33*(3), 303–318.

Moore, T. G. (1978). The Beneficiaries of Trucking Regulation. *Journal of Law and Transportation*, 21 (October), 327–343.

Nebesky, W., McMullen, S. B., & Lee, M.-K. (1995). Testing for Market Power in the U.S. Motor Carrier Industry. *Review of Industrial Organization*, *10*, 559–576.

Owen, D. S. (1988). Deregulation in the Trucking Industry. Economic Issues. Bureau of Economics, Federal Trade Commission (May).

Schumpeter, J. A. (1942). *Capitalism, Socialism and Democracy*. New York: Harper and Row.

Stigler, G. J. (1976). The Xistence of X-Efficiency. *American Economic Review* (March), 213–216.

Stevenson, R. (1980). Measuring Technological Bias. *American Economic Review*, *70*(1) (March), 162–173.

Thursby, M. Knox Lovell, C., & Blackorby, C. (1976). Notes and Memoranda: Extended Hicks Neutral Technical Change. *The Economic Journal*, *86* (December), 845–852.

U.S. General Accounting Office (1987). *Trucking Regulation: Price Competition and Market Structure in the Trucking Industry*. Washington, D.C. (February).

Wales, T. J. (1977). On The Flexibility of Flexible Functional Forms: An Empirical Approach. *Journal of Econometrics*, *5* (March), 183–193.

Winston, C. (1985). Conceptual Developments in the Economics of Transportation: An Interpretive Survey. *Journal of Economic Literature*, *23* (March), 83.

Winston, C., Corsi., T. M., Grimm, C. M., & Evans, C. A. (1990). *The Economic Effects of Surface Freight Deregulation*. Washington, D.C.: The Brookings Institution.

Ying, J. S. (1990a). Regulatory Reform and Technical Change: New Evidence of Scale Economies in Trucking. *Southern Economic Journal* (April), 996–1009.

Ying, J. S. (1990b). The inefficiency of Regulating a Competitive Industry: Productivity Gains in Trucking Following Reform. *Review of Economics and Statistics* (May), 91–201.

Ying, J. S., & Keeler, T. E. (1991). Pricing in a Deregulated Environment: the Motor Carrier Experience. *Rand Journal of Economics* (Summer), 264–273.

DEREGULATION AND WAGES IN TRUCKING: A TIME SERIES PHENOMENON – A TIME SERIES APPROACH

Kristen A. Monaco and Taggert J. Brooks

ABSTRACT

We approach measuring the wage effect of trucking deregulation from a new perspective using time series estimation techniques. The trucking wage is modeled as a function of the manufacturing wage and the relationship between these series is measured over time. We find that the wage premium of trucking over manufacturing is deterministic over time with two structural breaks in May 1980 and June 1984. This suggests that deregulation's effect on the trucking wage was mainly felt between 1980 and 1984. Using the relationship between the trucking wage and manufacturing wage before deregulation, we find that the initial effect of deregulation was to decrease wages 6.99%. This wage effect increased at a decreasing rate over time and by 1996 the cumulative effect was 12.43%.

Transportation After Deregulation, Volume 6, pages 55–69.

ISBN: 0-7623-0780-3

1. NON-STATIONARITY AND INDUSTRY ANALYSIS

Although much attention has been paid to non-stationarity in analyzing macroeconomic data, the same cannot be said of applied microeconomic analysis, particularly that which measures wages over time. Studies of the effects of government intervention rely largely on panel and repeated cross section data (often from the Current Population Survey).[1] Since these studies measure an intervention which is a non-discrete function of time (such as deregulation), it seems that particular attention should be paid to stochastic time processes in the data. However using cross-section and panel data, little attention has been paid to the data generating processes over time.

We postulate that analysis of deregulation could be done from a time series perspective. Rather than using cross-sectional observations on particular individuals over time, monthly time series data can be used to analyze industry changes. Trucking appears to be an ideal candidate, as most studies of deregulation's effect on trucking wages find significant wage decreases from deregulation. This makes trucking unlike telecommunications, airlines and railroads, where deregulation's effect was felt primarily through employment and not wages (Hendricks, 1994). Studies on trends in trucking wages over the past 20 years have few, if any, time controls, however, trucking deregulation began administratively in the mid to late 1970s and was enacted as law in 1980, a period when there were also strong downward trends in blue collar wages economy-wide.

Though trucking wages fell following deregulation (using 1979 as a benchmark as is common to trucking studies), the downward trends in driver wages preceded this and are mirrored in movements of manufacturing wages (used as a proxy for economy-wide wage trends), see Fig. 1. It is clearly the case that using only a dummy variable to measure deregulation, absent any other time controls, may substantially overstate deregulation's effect. Trucking wage declines found in previous studies may compound deregulation's effect with downward pressure on wages unrelated to deregulation.

Using time series econometric techniques we compare declines in the trucking wage to the manufacturing wage. We can identify periods where the real wage differential between trucking and manufacturing is deterministic, and the points in time where there is a structural break in the differential. Though a structural break could be caused by many factors, such as technology or aggregate demand shocks exclusive to an industry, the structural break of particular interest to this study is deregulation. The goal is to determine whether deregulation explains the change in the trucking wage vis-à-vis a non-regulated industry. A further innovation is that we make no a priori assumptions about the dating of deregulation's impact.

Relying on tests of stationarity we find that the average hourly trucking and manufacturing wage are consistent with a unit root, and therefore not mean reverting. However, the premium of the trucking wage over the manufacturing wage appears to be a deterministic (trend stationary) series with two structural breaks, one at May 1980 and the other at June 1984. This suggests that the relationship between trucking and manufacturing wages, while having fundamentally changed around the time of deregulation, is otherwise predictable. Using the pre and post deregulation trucking premium to forecast the trucking wage we find that in 1980 (month 5) deregulation accounted for a 6.99% decrease in the trucking wage and by 1996 (month 2) a 12.43% decrease in the average hourly wage in the trucking industry.

2. DEREGULATION OF MOTOR CARRIAGE

Regulation of trucking was legislated with the passage of the 1935 Motor Carrier Act, resulting in rents to the industry through entry restrictions and price fixing through rate bureaus. Moore (1978) refers to regulation as "carteliz[ing] the industry" (p. 328). Administrative deregulation was begun by the Interstate Commerce Commission in the late 1970s with the loosening of entry restrictions. The administrative changes of the ICC were passed as law with the 1980 Motor Carrier Act, which also eliminated rate bureaus.

The literature on deregulation's effect on trucking concentrates on two distinct areas: cost and wages. On the operations side, one would expect firm costs to decrease following deregulation as rate bureaus were eliminated and entry allowed, resulting in a more competitive industry structure (McMullen, 1989). Indeed, motor carriage saw just this change. The post-deregulation period was characterized by upheaval among trucking firms, with many established firms leaving the market and the emergence of smaller firms. Studies which examine the effect of deregulation on firm costs typically use the benchmark of 1977 as the beginning of the post-deregulation period, with the justification that since administrative deregulation began prior to the passage of the Motor Carrier Act, effects on industry structure and costs undoubtedly began earlier than 1980.

The second body of literature which examines deregulation's effect centers on the labor market. Since the higher rates and restricted entry pre-deregulation resulted in industry rents, it is reasonable to hypothesize that these rents might be shared with workers. The existence of industry rents along with the strength of the Teamsters union seem to explain the relatively high wages in the unionized segment of the trucking labor force during the regulated period. Wages of non-union workers in trucking were not appreciably different than those of manufacturing workers indicating that the rent-sharing was not experienced by the non-union sector, nor is there evidence of appreciable threat effects. As an illustration, the mean hourly wages of drivers in the trucking industry in 1974 were \$13.99 for union, \$9.47 for non-union, versus \$9.48 for manufacturing workers (reported in 1982–1984 dollars) (Belman & Monaco, forthcoming).

As the industry moved to a more competitive environment post-deregulation, wages fell precipitously. In 1984 the mean hourly wages of drivers in the trucking industry were \$11.09 for union and \$7.93 for non-union, compared to the mean manufacturing wage of \$9.02. Not surprising, given the presumed rent-sharing in the union segment of the industry, union drivers were those affected most by deregulation. Rose (1987) and Hirsch (1988) find that deregulation lowered wages of union drivers on the order of 15%, using data from the Current Population Survey. Belzer (1994), using firm-level data, finds a 20% wage decline due to deregulation across workers. The wage studies typically use a benchmark of 1979 as the start of the post-deregulation period, again theorizing that deregulation's effect in labor markets was felt in the period of administrative deregulation, prior to the Motor Carrier Act of 1980.

3. ESTIMATION OF THE RELATIONSHIP BETWEEN WAGES

Approaching the analysis deregulation's effect on trucking wages from a time series perspective first requires some explanation of time series data analysis.[2] The bulk of univariate time series analysis involves forecasting:

$$y_t = \alpha y_{t-1} + \mu + \beta_t + \varepsilon_t \qquad (1)$$

where y is the series of interest, μ is the intercept term, t represents a linear time trend and ε_t is a stochastic error term.

There are basically three types of series, mean stationary, trend stationary, and non-stationary (unit root). A mean stationary series, upon deviation from its mean, tends to revert to the mean. In Eq. (1) this would imply α is less than one and β is zero. If a series is mean stationary then the series will revert back to its mean after any shock (positive or negative value of t). A trend stationary process fluctuates about a linear, or deterministic, trend. This would imply that in Eq. (1), is less than one and takes a value other than zero. A shock to a trend stationary series will dissipate over time and the series will eventually revert to its trend. The final type, a unit root series, does not revert to a mean or a linear trend. This implies that is equal to one and μ and can take any value zero or otherwise. Any shock to the series permanently alters the forecast by the full amount of the shock.

In the context of our analysis, we compare the wages of drivers in the trucking industry to workers in manufacturing. The manufacturing wage was chosen for two reasons. First, we have reason to expect that it can be considered a "reservation wage" for truck drivers as these groups have similar demographic characteristics. Second, there is no reason to expect that trucking deregulation should have any significant effect on the wages in manufacturing.

Figure 1 shows trends in the average hourly wages for these two industries (deflated with the monthly CPI-U in 1982–1984 dollars) from the first month of 1972 to the second month of 1996. The data source used is "Employment, Hours, and Earnings United States, 1909–1994" and "Employment, Hours, and Earnings United States, 1995–1996," published by the U.S. Department of Labor. As is evident, the trucking wage has declined in real terms over time, but these declines are particularly significant beginning in the late 1970s, which also corresponds to the beginning of deregulation. However it is interesting to note that the manufacturing wage also declined precipitously over the same period.

The series of interest is the natural log of the wage differential between truckers and manufacturing workers. This captures the percentage wage premium of drivers (who consistently earn higher wages). Given that labor is fairly mobile between industries, there are two possible explanations for the wage differentials between trucking and manufacturing: skill differentials and compensating differentials. However a major source of the trucking wage premium prior to 1980 was regulation. Rent sharing was prevalent in trucking pre-deregulation, especially for unionized drivers. (Hirsch, 1988 and Rose, 1987).

Looking at changes in the wage premium of trucking over manufacturing across time should provide insight into the effects of deregulation, as we assume that the two groups feel economy-wide macroeconomic shocks in a proportionate manner. A graph of the seasonally adjusted wage premium is presented in Fig. 2. Thus, economy-wide declining unionization[3] and declining real wages should be felt by both groups of workers, thus not significantly affecting the wage differential. This differential would be expected to change given shocks that were felt solely by workers in one industry – trucking deregulation would be one of these shocks.

Changes in the wage premium over time should allow us to infer deregulation's effect. The first step is to analyze this series and determine whether it is stationary, both over the entire time period and within sub-periods (i.e. before and after deregulation). Stationarity would imply a long run stability of the wage premium of trucking over manufacturing. A theoretically appealing result would be to find this series stationary about distinct means before and after deregulation, implying a stable wage premium of trucking, then measure the

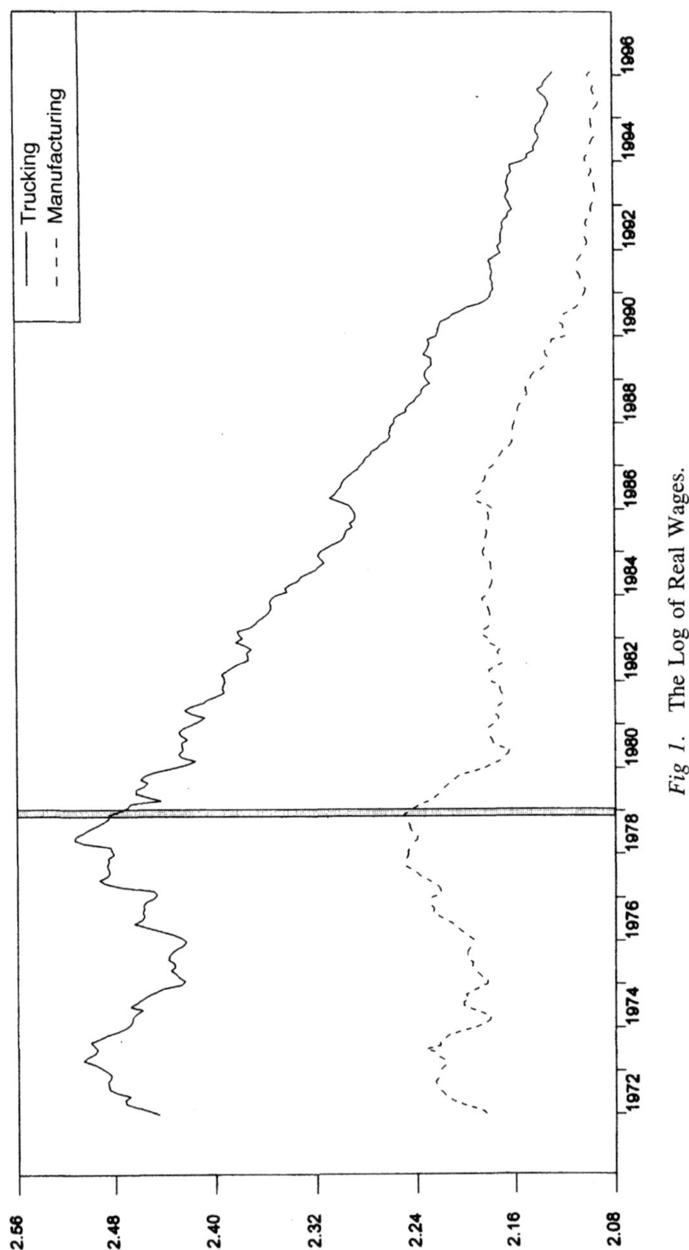

Fig 1. The Log of Real Wages.

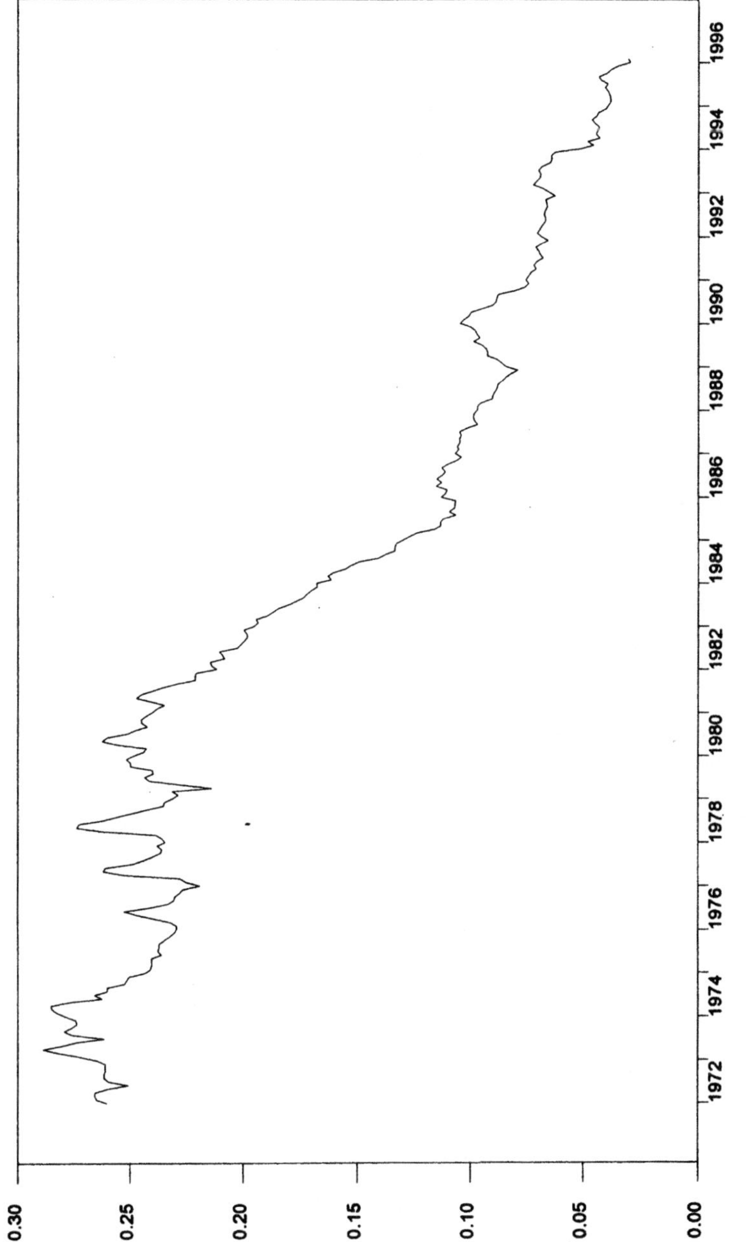

Fig 2. Log of Trucking Wage Premium.

difference in means in the premium between these periods, ostensibly a good proxy for deregulation's effect.

4. DISCUSSION OF UNIT ROOTS

A brief review of unit root tests is provided, as background for interpreting the tables and the implications of the tests for measuring deregulation's effect. A non-stationary series is integrated of order one if its first difference is stationary and reverts to a mean. However, it is not necessarily the case that a unit root characterizes all non-stationary series; non-stationary series could either be trend or difference stationary, the latter the only case that implies the presence of a unit root. To test for the type of stationarity present in the series of the wage premium, we implement two unit root tests. These are the Augmented Dickey-Fuller (ADF) and Kwiatkowski, Phillips, Schmidt and Shin (KPSS) tests.[4,5]

The KPSS relies upon a Lagrange Multiplier test with the null hypothesis of stationarity (trend or difference). For the test of level stationarity it decomposes the process to a random walk and stationary error, and incorporates a deterministic trend to test trend stationarity. The variance of the random walk component is tested, with a null hypothesis of zero variance. The test has one choice parameter, the lag truncation variable associated with the weighting spectral window. We use the Bartlett window as suggested in Kwiatkowski et al. (1992), but use an agnostic approach to the choice of lag parameter due to the size and power distortions inherent in finite samples.

As the ADF and KPSS tests have contrasting null hypotheses (the null of ADF is non-stationarity and the null of KPSS is stationarity) there are four possible outcomes from performing hypothesis tests (Cheung and Chinn, 1994 and forthcoming). The first consists of "accepting" (failing to reject) the null hypothesis for both tests, which tends to occur due to the lack of power of the tests in small samples. The second consists of rejecting the null of KPSS and "accepting" the null of ADF, corresponding to a robust acceptance of the existence of a unit root. The third, where the null of ADF is rejected and the null of KPSS is "accepted" is a robust acceptance of stationarity. Finding stationarity over the entire time period would have suggested that the wage premium of trucking over manufacturing was stable across the entire time period, suggesting no wage effect of deregulation.

5. RESULTS

Table 1 reports the results of the KPSS and ADF tests for the full sample. The ADF test statistic for the trucking wage premium is −2.65 and that of the KPSS

Table 1. Unit Root Test on Full Sample 1972:1 to 1996:2.

	ADF	KPSS
Manufacturing (15)	–3.05	0.614
Trucking (14)	–2.38	0.786
Truck premium (13)	–2.65	0.544

* The lag for the ADF test was selected using the Akaike Information Criterion (AIC) and it appears in parenthesis behind the series name. The critical values for the ADF test are –3.98 at the 1% level, –3.42 at the 5% level, and –3.13 at the 10% level. The KPSS test reports the ETA(tau) test statistic when 4 lags are used with the Bartlett window. The critical values are 0.216 at the 1% level, 0.146 at the 5% level, and 0.119 at the 10% level.

is 0.544, which when compared to the critical values given leads us to reject the hypothesis of stationarity. As we do not find stationarity over the entire time period, we next test the wage premium for the presence of a structural break. A trend stationary process with a structural break is often indistinguishable from a difference stationary process (Perron, 1989). If the wage differential could be represented by a stationary process with a structural break corresponding to deregulation then the difference in means would capture the wage effect of deregulation. A recent unit root test by Perron (1997) allows for endogenous determination of the break point. This is especially important with the data on trucking, as the actual date of deregulation is hard to determine – Motor Carrier Act of 1980 represented the legal deregulation of trucking, however administrative deregulation preceded this. Many studies use 1979 as the date of deregulation.[6]

Perron's test involves is similar to the Dickey-Fuller test and involves estimating equation 2.

$$y_t = \alpha y_{t-1} + \mu + \theta DU_t + \beta_t + \gamma DT_t + \delta D(T_b)_t + \sum_{i=1}^{k} c_i \Delta y_{t-i} + e_t \qquad (1)$$

Where y is again the series of interest, μ is the constant term, t incorporates a time trend, e is a stochastic time component, and is the date of the structural break The variable DU is a dummy variable which takes a value of one after the structural break and D(Tb)t is a variable which takes a value of one in the period immediately following the structural break. Finally, DTt takes a value of t for the period after the structural break; allowing the slope as well as the intercept to change following the structural break. The unit root test involves using the t statistic to test $\alpha = 1$. A rejection of the null hypothesis suggests that the series is stationary around a structural break.

The results of applying this test to the trucking premium can be found in Table 2, where the structural break is dated as 1980, month 5 (May). This is interesting as it is closer to the actual passage of the MCA in October 1980 than the structural break of 1979 used in cross-sectional studies. However, the trucking premium is still non-stationary, since we fail to reject the null hypothesis. One potential reason for this finding could be the existence of yet another structural break. Table 3 presents the results of unit root tests on the data series before 1980:5 and while not robust, do to the low power of the truncated sample, they do suggest that this period was stationary. The ADF statistic of 3.11 is very close to the 10% critical value of the test statistic which would allow us to reject the null of non-stationarity. This suggests that the source of non-stationarity stems from the series post 1980:5. Visual inspection of Fig. 2 suggests that another structural break occurred in the mid 80s. Applying Perron's test to the data after focusing on the post deregulation data (post 1980:5), we find that indeed the trucking premium is stationary after allowing for a structural break at 1984:6. The results of Perron's test are presented in Table 4. Tables 5 and 6 confirm this result using the KPSS and ADF tests on the sub samples. Table 5 presents the ADF and KPSS statistics on the trucking wage premium for the period 1980:5 through 1984:5. The test statistic of the ADF of −3.28

Table 2. Perron's Unit Root Test on Full Sample 1972:1 to 1996:2.

	Break Point	alpha	t-stat (alpha = 1)
Truck premium (12)	1980:5	0.965	−2.22

* The model allowed for both a change in the intercept and a change in the trend and the critical values are −5.57 at the 1% level, −4.91 at the 5% level, and −4.59 at the 10% level.

Table 3. Unit Root Test on 1972:1 to 1980:4.

	ADF	KPSS
Manufacturing (15)	−2.61	0.192
Trucking (13)	−4.21	0.203
Truck premium (1)	−3.11	0.202

* The lag for the ADF test was selected using the Akaike Information Criterion (AIC) and it appears in parenthesis behind the series name. The critical values for the ADF test are −3.98 at the 1% level, −3.42 at the 5% level, and −3.13 at the 10% level. The KPSS test reports the ETA(tau) test statistic when 4 lags are used with the Bartlett window. The critical values are 0.216 at the 1% level, 0.146 at the 5% level, and 0.119 at the 10% level.

Table 4. Perron's Unit Root Test on Full Sample 1980:5 to 1996:2.

	Break Point	alpha	t-stat (alpha = 1)
Truck premium (6)	1984:6	0.853	−4.66

* The model allowed for both a change in the intercept and a change in the trend and the critical values are −5.57 at the 1% level, −4.91 at the 5% level, and −4.59 at the 10% level.

Table 5. Unit Root Test on 1980:5 to 1984:5.

	ADF	KPSS
Manufacturing (0)	−2.48	0.073
Trucking (19)	−1.67	0.059
Truck premium(3)	−3.28	0.072

* The lag for the ADF test was selected using the Akaike Information Criterion (AIC) and it appears in parenthesis behind the series name. The critical values for the ADF test are −3.98 at the 1% level, −3.42 at the 5% level, and −3.13 at the 10% level. The KPSS test reports the ETA(tau) test statistic when 4 lags are used with the Bartlett window. The critical values are 0.216 at the 1% level, 0.146 at the 5% level, and 0.119 at the 10% level.

Table 6. Unit Root Test on 1984:6 to 1996:2.

	ADF	KPSS
Manufacturing (1)	−1.29	0.482
Trucking (2)	−2.41	0.352
Truck premium(3)	−3.76	0.125

* The lag for the ADF test was selected using the Akaike Information Criterion (AIC) and it appears in parenthesis behind the series name. The critical values for the ADF test are −3.98 at the 1% level, −3.42 at the 5% level, and −3.13 at the 10% level. The KPSS test reports the ETA(tau) test statistic when 4 lags are used with the Bartlett window. The critical values are 0.216 at the 1% level, 0.146 at the 5% level, and 0.119 at the 10% level.

allows us to reject the null hypothesis of a unit root at the 10% level. The KPSS test statistic of 0.072 means we fail to reject the null hypothesis of no unit root. Recall from the discussion on unit roots that this combination of results allows a robust acceptance of stationarity. The same acceptance of stationarity holds for the period 1984:6 through 1996:2 as evidenced in Table 6. We reject the null of the ADF at the 5% level with a test statistic of −3.76

and fail to reject the null hypothesis of the KPSS test at the 5% level with a statistic of 0.125.

Our findings suggest that the relationship between the average hourly manufacturing wage and the average hourly trucking wage as measured by the wage premium has been deterministic, that is to say it has fluctuated around a linear with two different break points. The first break point occurs in the fifth month of 1980 and the second occurs in the sixth month of 1984. It is important to note that in all cases the premium was trending downward implying a convergence in wages. If we use the deterministic trend in the wage premium prior to 1980:5 and the trend in the wage premium after 1984:6 we can infer the effects of deregulation.[7] Figure 3 represents this graphically. If we attribute this entire reduction in the premium to a reduction in the average hourly wages in the trucking industry we can then calculate the percentage reduction in hourly wages due to deregulation.

In 1980:5 deregulation accounted for a 6.99% decline in the average hourly wages of truck drivers and by 1984:6 that percent had climbed to 8.42%. In February of 1996, the last date for which we have data, the average hourly wage of truck drivers is 12.43% lower then it might otherwise have been. Our findings suggest that previous studies attribute too much of the observed wage declines to deregulation, when in fact some of it stems from factors experienced by other unregulated industries, such as manufacturing. These factors can include, but are not limited to the recession in the early 80s, the rapid appreciation of the dollar brought on by the monetary aggregate targeting, and the increase in the trade deficit.

6. CONCLUSIONS

Our findings suggest that the average hourly wages earned in the trucking industry and the manufacturing industry have enjoyed a predictable relationship since 1972. The relationship is only predictable after accounting for two break points, the first in 1980:5 and the second in 1984:6. Therefore one can think of the impact of deregulation occurring over the middle period from 1980:6 to 1984:5, rather then simply a discrete point in time, such as 1979:1. During this period the trucking industry experienced a rapid attrition of firms in the Less then Truckload (LTL) (high wage) segment, some through failure others through mergers, while the Truckload (TL) (low wage) segment witnessed an explosion in small firms (Burks, 1999).

Many cross-sectional studies of trucking find a wage effect of deregulation on the order of 20% or more (Belzer, 1994, Hirsch, 1988). These studies include only a discrete dummy variable for deregulation and no controls for macroeco-

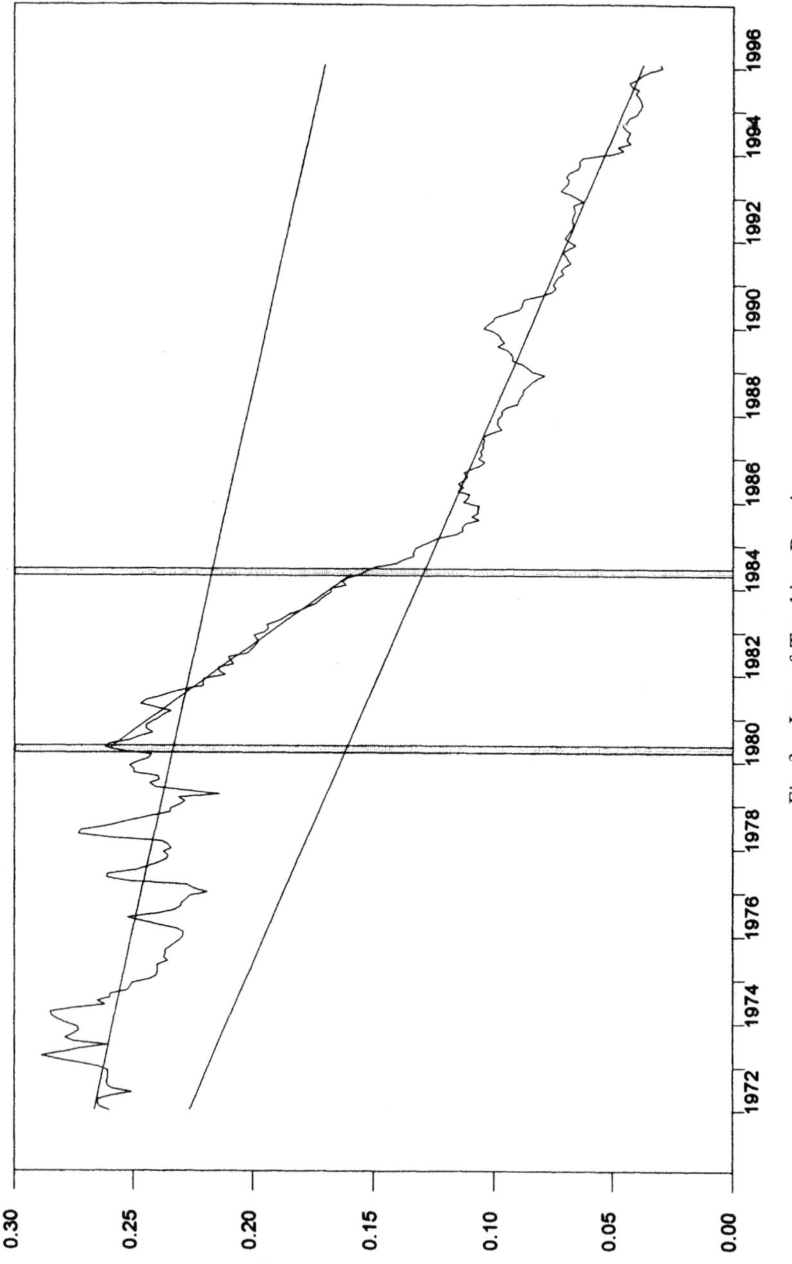

Fig 3. Log of Trucking Premium.

nomic effects. Using the period before deregulation to predict the trucking wage into the other period we find that deregulation accounts for a 6.99% decline in trucking wages in 1980:5 and by 1996:2 that effect compounds to a 12.34% reduction in wages. We find that the effect of deregulation is felt later than previously assumed and, rather than occurring at a discrete point in time, has accumulated over time, with the primary effect felt between 1980:5 and 1984:6.

NOTES

1. Examples are numerous. Cites for the trucking industry alone include Rose (1987), Hirsch (1988, 1993), Heywood and Peoples (1994) and Peoples and Saunders (1993).
2. For a more complete analysis of stationary and non-stationary series refer to Greene (1997, pp. 841–851) and Harvey (1993, pp. 10–11).
3. It can be argued however, that, although both groups experienced declining wages due to de-unionization, deregulation accelerated this de-unionization in the trucking industry and thus it is very difficult to fully disentangle deregulation effects from de-unionization effects for this group.
4. For the ADF the optimal lag length is chosen using the Akaike Information Criterion (AIC).
5. For a discussion of these tests see Cheung and Chinn (1994).
6. For example, Belzer (1994), Rose (1987) and Hirsch (1988, 1993).
7. The equations for these lines are obtained by regressing the trucking wage premium on a constant term and trend term within the period under consideration. For the period 1972:1–1980:4 the resulting equation is $y(t) = 0.295 - 0.0003t$. For the period 1984:6–1992:2 the equation is $y(t) = 0.282 - 0.00065t$. Full estimation results are available from the authors upon request.

ACKNOWLEDGMENTS

The authors would like to acknowledge the generous support of the University of Michigan Trucking Industry Program, funded by a grant from the Alfred P. Sloan Foundation. We would also like to thank Norman Morin, Phil Rothman, G. Colletaz and F. Serranito for providing their RATS code.

REFERENCES

Belzer, M. (1994). The Motor Carriage Industry: Truckers and Teamsters under Seige. In: P. Voos (Ed.), *Contemporary Collective Bargaining* (pp. 259–302). Ithaca: ILR Press.

Belman, D. L., & Monaco, K. A. (forthcoming). How Did Truck Drivers' Jobs Become So Bad? The Effects of Deregulation, Technology and Human Capital. *Industrial and Labor Relations Review*.

Burks, S. V. (1999). Product Market Segmentation in Motor Freight: A Survival Analysis of Firm Specialization after Deregulation. University of Michigan Trucking Industry Program Working Paper.

Cheung, Y., & Chinn, M. D. (forthcoming). Deterministic, Stochastic, and Segmented Trend in Aggregate Output: A Cross-Country Analysis. Oxford Economics Papers.

Enders, W. (1995). *Applied Econometric Time Series.* New York: John Wiley and Sons.

Engle, R., & Granger, C. W. J. (1987). Co-integration and Error Correction: Representation, Estimation, and Testing. *Econometrica, 55,* 251–276.

Granger, C. W. J., & Newbold, P. (1974). Spurious Regression in Econometrics. *Journal of Econometrics, 2,* 111–120.

Greene, W. (1997). *Econometric Analysis* (3rd ed.). Upper Saddle River, NJ: Prentice Hall.

Harvey, A. C. (1993). *Time Series Analysis* (2nd ed.). Cambridge: MIT Press.

Hendricks, W. (1994). Deregulation and Labor Earnings. *Journal of Labor Research, 15,* 209–234.

Heywood, J., & Peoples, J. (1994). Deregulation and the Prevalence of Black Truck Drivers. *Journal of Law and Economics, 37,* 133–155.

Hirsch, B. (1988). Trucking Regulation, Unionization and Labor Earnings: 1973–1985. *Journal of Human Resources, 23,* 296–319.

Hirsch, B. (1993). Trucking Deregulation and Labor Earnings: Is the Union Premium a Compensating Differential? *Journal of Labor Economics, 11,* 279–301.

Kwiatkowski, D., Phillips, P. C. B., Schmidt, P., & Shin, Y. (1992). Testing the Null Hypothesis of Stationarity against the Alternative of a Unit Root. *Journal of Econometrics, 54,* 159–178.

McMullen, B. S. (1989). The Impact of Regulatory Reform on U.S. Motor Carrier Costs. *Journal of Transport Economics and Policy,* 307–319.

Peoples, J., & Saunders, L. (1993). Trucking Deregulation and the Black/White Wage Gap. *Industrial and Labor Relations Review, 47,* 23–35.

Perron, P. (1989). The Great Crash, the Oil Price Shock, and the Unit Root Hypothesis. *Econometrica, 57,* 1361–1401.

Perron, P. (1997). Further Evidence on the Breaking Trend Functions in Macroeconomic Variables. *Journal of Econometrics, 80,* 355–385.

Phillips, P. C. B. (1986). Understanding Spurious Regression in Econometrics. *Journal of Econometrics, 33,* 311–340.

Rose, N. (1987). Labor Rent Sharing and Regulation: Evidence from the Trucking Industry. Journal of Political Economy, 95, 1146–1178.

U.S. Department of Labor (1994). *Employment, Hours and Earnings United States, 1909–1994.*

U.S. Department of Labor (1996). *Employment, Hours and Earnings United States, 1995–1996.*

MARKETING STRATEGY AND THE USE OF INFORMATION TECHNOLOGY: NEW EVIDENCE FROM THE TRUCKING INDUSTRY

Atreya Chakraborty and Mark Kazarosian

ABSTRACT

Since the mid-1980s, many authors have investigated the influence of information technology (IT) on productivity. Until recently there has been no clear evidence that productivity increases as a result of IT spending. This productivity paradox is partly due to the difficulty in correctly identifying outputs, particularly in a service sector such as the trucking industry. Products are often differentiated by quality attributes of the service provided, rather than merely the physical content of the good delivered by motor carriers. A carrier's primary marketing objective, e.g. on-time performance vs. lowest-rate carrier, is precisely what differentiates a trucking firm's service. This paper uses cross-sectional data to show that the use of increasingly sophisticated IT by trucking firms varies depending upon marketing objectives. Our empirical results imply that, in order to measure the impact of IT on productivity, it is crucial to account for how the firm differentiates its product. We conclude that the productivity paradox can be alleviated if measures of output incorporate firms' marketing objectives.

Transportation After Deregulation, Volume 6, pages 71–96.
2001 by Elsevier Science Ltd.
ISBN: 0-7623-0780-3

1. INTRODUCTION

Did a university's 1980 investment in new Vax computers help faculty and students be more productive? Does investment in a satellite communications network improve the productivity of UPS workers? Ten years ago, the answers to similar questions were either "maybe" or "no," and this productivity paradox of information technology (IT) fueled a large body of literature.[1]

Brynjolfsson and Hitt (1998) summarize the key reasons for the productivity paradox with the following humorous passage:

> Productivity is a simple concept. It is the amount of output produced per unit of input [yet productivity] is notoriously difficult to measure ... In particular, there are two aspects of productivity that have increasingly defied precise measurement: output and input.

More recently, better data and a clearer understanding of how to measure both outputs and inputs have begun to reveal that use of technology may in fact improve productivity. Using cross-sectional data, this paper finds that the use of increasingly sophisticated IT by trucking firms depends on marketing objectives. Marketing objectives are defined by a firm's competitive strategy, and these objectives are met by product differentiation. Our empirical results imply that, in order to measure output precisely, it is crucial to account for how a firm differentiates its product.

Evidence of a connection between a firm's use of IT and its marketing objectives would suggest that these traditionally intangible variables add a new dimension to the firm's measured output. If this is true, then productivity studies (even at the firm level) may need to include the firm's objectives to identify output correctly. Measured output can no longer be limited to simply counting widgets.

Measures of productivity – defined as the effect of IT on output – must incorporate a firm's competitive strategies. This connection of IT with competitive strategy is important for understanding one of many reasons the productivity paradox initially existed. Suppose two trucking firms provide the (seemingly) exact same service – the delivery of heavy machinery. Yet one firm has on-time performance as its most important objective, while the other firm markets itself as having the lowest freight rate. Each firm uses IT differently depending on how each markets its service, even though both may deliver one machine per day. If output is measured as the number of machines delivered, the relationship between productivity and IT use will be mis-measured. The on-time performer delivering an asphalt spreader to a construction site two hours late can count its output as zero. The lowest-rate carrier moves that same spreader when it is idle from one storage site to another. If that delivery is a few hours late it is still a productive day. The on-time performer will differentiate its service – timely delivery of the spreader – by using sophisticated IT. The lowest-rate firm has little need for the same technology. Production studies that aggregate over all firms delivering heavy machinery will not accurately gauge the true impact of IT.

The difficulty of measuring output in the face of accelerating use of technology is clearly important in the modern economy, yet the existing empirical literature is in its early stages. Until now, data sets containing both detailed output and financial characteristics, as well as particular types of firm-specific technologies, have been hard to find. Even with the recent availability of firm-level data explored by Brynjolfsson and Hitt (1996), and detailed truck-level data explored by Hubbard (1998), the issue of how to measure output precisely still has not been fully explored. We do not attempt to measure productivity in this paper, but we do uncover evidence indicating that, given the use of IT to differentiate a firm's product, marketing objectives must be taken into account when measuring output.

We use a new data set that contains information about firms' objectives, detailed technology use, and financial and operating characteristics. Our probit and ordered probit estimations explain the use of three levels of technological sophistication. The groups of technology that reflect intensity are intuitively straightforward. The categories are: (1) no technology, (2) two-way radios, cell phones, or pagers, and (3) automatic vehicle location (AVL) systems, on-board-computers, or satellite communications.[2] We test whether IT use responds to truckers' haul characteristics differently depending upon the firm's primary marketing objective.[3] The empirical models control for key variables, including complementary technologies, operating characteristics, financial attributes, and industrywide organizational structure. Our models distinguish between information-gathering technologies (dependent variable) and information-processing technologies (explanatory variable).[4]

Our results show that a firm's marketing objective is a key factor in determining the patterns of IT use. Haul characteristics have a statistically significant influence on IT use for firms with a primary marketing objective of on-time performance. For those firms not concerned with on-time performance, this is not the case. We infer from these results that two firms could be delivering the same product, yet be using different levels of technology owing to the particular market niche they have carved. A firm's choice to use sophisticated IT depends more upon the way a product is delivered (e.g. on-time versus lowest freight rate) rather than *what* product is delivered. Moreover, the patterns of IT use that we observe suggest that the number of products delivered is not the only component of the measured output. We take these results as evidence that output measures should incorporate the firm-specific objective that reflects the customer's perception of a successfully delivered good.

After a summary of the related literature and a brief description of the trucking industry in Section 2, Section 3 presents the empirical implementation. Section 4 describes the data, Section 5 the results and implications, and Section 6 offers concluding remarks.

2. LITERATURE REVIEW AND THE TRUCKING INDUSTRY

Porter (1985a, b, c) lays the groundwork for understanding the complex relationship between a firm's use of IT and the nature of that firm's output. Firms *must* adopt some forms of IT just to survive in a quickly changing environment. Technology changes industry structure, creates competitive advantage, spawns completely new businesses, and literally transforms industries by actuating new approaches to competitive behavior. Firms are increasingly able to customize products to serve small market niches; thus, IT enhances a company's ability to differentiate itself. Products have been reshaped by the use of IT, and the product's definition must now include multidimensional quality characteristics. In the trucking industry, such characteristics would include whether trucks deliver products on time or at the lowest freight rate.

Porter recognized early that the influence of IT on the modern economy would make it difficult to pin down a precise definition of the firm's output. Indeed a "productivity paradox" emerged in 1980s literature, and this paradox, in no small part, reflected Porter's observations that output, transformed by IT, would be difficult to measure for many reasons. Roach (1987) and Solow (1987) first recognized this paradox – no clear evidence of productivity increases as a result of IT spending. Their premature conclusions, summarized by Solow's statement that "we see the computer age everywhere except in the productivity statistics," were based on early and aggregate data. As Porter implicitly predicted, it was too early for the data to reveal the true long-term benefits of IT – production processes do not change overnight. Also, even if the IT benefits existed, they were washed out in the aggregate data.

The ensuing research that investigates the influence of IT on a firm's performance is large and is reviewed by Brynjolfsson (1993) and Wilson (1993). The results from these studies are mixed, suggesting positive, negative, and zero effects of the use of technology on productivity. The assorted results can be only partly explained by problems stemming from the use of aggregate data (Morrison & Berndt, 1990), small sample size of firm-level data (Loveman, 1994), unreliable data (Siegel & Griliches, 1991), or misspecifications, such as using profits as performance measures (Dos Santos et al., 1993). More recently, examinations of large, firm-level time-series data by Brynjolfsson and Hitt

(1995, 1996), Lichtenberg (1995), and Dewan and Min (1997) indicate that IT might enhance productivity.

Even after careful investigation of representative microdata, a nagging question remains – what reflects the true output of the firm? In today's highly specialized economy, particularly in the service sector, output is certainly more than merely the number of widgets produced. Instead, to measure output, one must take into account the value provided to the customer. Brynjolfsson and Hitt (1996) acknowledge that there is "an inherent difficulty of measuring the benefits of IT investment." Recognizing this, they queried managers to determine their justifications for investing in IT. The most important reasons were customer service, cost savings, timeliness, and quality. Indeed, Brynjolfsson and Hitt (1995) suggest that future research examine subsamples of IT data based on organizational form and management strategy. This paper does precisely that by exploring how the use of IT varies in response to the manager's perception of what is important (e.g. timeliness).

A clear illustration of the difficulty in defining output as a result of IT can be found in the trucking industry. Trucking offers a prime test case since, as in any service industry, several nonphysical components constitute a firm's output. Also, the industry has recently become technologically intensive, and technology use is heterogeneous.

Deregulation legislated by the Motor Carrier Act of 1980 stimulated competition among previously unrelated trucking firms. The Interstate Commerce Commission (ICC) eased its strict entry policy by granting operating certificates at an accelerated rate. Because of this open-door policy, along with more flexible carrier rates, the industry experienced a drastic restructuring and reorganization (Grimm et al., 1989, Zingales, 1998, Hubbard, 1998). Truckers could now haul goods relatively unfettered by previously constraining regulations. The availability and proliferation of IT throughout the trucking industry coincided with this deregulation. New and existing firms needed to carve out niches, i.e. differentiate their products by offering services related to their "core competence" or comparative advantage.

Zingales (1998) finds that both the fittest (economically efficient) as well as the fattest (substantially liquid) trucking firms survived the deregulation. IT such as cellular phones and electronic data interchange (EDI), coupled with deregulation, played an important role at this time by enabling entry into otherwise untouchable markets. Smaller (or newly entering) firms that perhaps did not have the financial ability to buy sophisticated technology were forced to be the fittest and specialize along a different path than the larger firms. Firms with the ability to borrow more easily or with more cash availability (the fattest) could more quickly adopt the sophisticated and expensive technologies, such as satellite communications.

Porter's insight that IT use would make output difficult to measure is particularly important in the trucking industry and is highlighted by the findings of Zingales (1998). Zingales investigates the increased risk of bankruptcy in the post-deregulation trucking industry. Surviving firms were among the fittest and the fattest, and were precisely those that adjusted their operating routines to the changing needs of the industry. The adjustment of operating routines was often associated with the adoption of IT to gain a market niche and exploit a firm's core competence. This dynamic market made it *increasingly* difficult to measure output and, consequently, the productivity resulting from IT investment.

Hubbard (1998) investigates where and why IT is valuable in the trucking industry. He uses truck-level data to explore how the use of two types of on-board computers are influenced by detailed carrier, shipper, and haul information. He finds that trip recorders, a technology that enables incentive benefits, are more common on trucks operating far from home, making fewer stops, within private fleets, and on trucks that are under longer-term use agreements.[5] Electronic vehicle management systems (EVMS) (associated with coordination benefits) are more common as haul-length increases, within for-hire fleets, and on trucks that are under longer-term use agreements.

Our investigation is similar to Hubbard (1998) in that both papers explore the determinants of IT use. Yet we ask a different question, owing to our access to information about the firm's marketing objectives, more detailed technology data, and the firm's financial characteristics. Hubbard's finding that both incentive- and coordination-related benefits make IT valuable complement our finding that IT use depends upon the firm's marketing objectives. For example, the goal of being an on-time performer (a key variable in our investigation) is certainly closely related to *both* incentive – and coordination-related benefits of IT. Hubbard did not explicitly consider how his results related to productivity, yet those results support our conclusion. The firm needs to be concerned with *both* incentive- and coordination-related benefits of IT in order to meet its objective of being on time.

3. THE EMPIRICAL MODEL

We observe the use of IT in discrete amounts. For example, either a trucking firm uses cell phones or it does not. Yet the need for technology in production is truly a continuous, unobserved (latent) variable. This variable – the sophistication of IT use – is determined by a firm's operational characteristics and marketing objectives. We model this latent variable in two ways. The latent variable has either one observed threshold (a probit model) or two observed thresholds (an ordered probit model). Each threshold denotes the transition from one set of technologies to another. As the firm crosses a higher threshold, more sophisticated technologies are used. Our goal is to identify empirically both these thresholds and the firms' characteristics that affect the observed use of technology.

Our first specification, the probit model, captures a simplistic view of adopting IT. In this world, the firms are either high- or low-technology users. High technologies are state-of-the-art information-gathering technologies that include satellite communications (SATCOM), on-board computers (OBC), or AVL and tracking devices.[6] Low technologies are basic communication technologies that include two-way radios, cell phones, or pagers. The low-technology group in this specification also includes firms using none of the above communication technologies. These firms perhaps depend upon local telephone networks.

Our second approach, the ordered probit, recognizes that firms using no communication technologies whatsoever may have very different operational characteristics than their counterparts using even the most basic gadgets. Hubbard (1998) investigates a problem similar to ours and uses a multinomial logit. His three categories distinguish firms with no technology from those with trip recorders and those with EVMS. We have grouped and ordered our six information-gathering technologies according to their sophistication (see Table 3). For example, a satellite communications network gathers more information than a two-way radio and is in the high-technology category. Using an ordered probit helps us to capture this inherent ordering of the sophistication of IT use.

Both of our empirical specifications are summarized here. The probit model simply collapses the first two categories of the ordered probit, presented below, into one category.

$t_i = \beta' X_i + \varepsilon$

$y = 1$ if no IT is used, i.e. $t_i \leq 0$

$y = 2$ if only CELL or CB or PAGER, i.e. $t_i \leq \mu_1$

$y = 3$ if OBC or AVL or SATCOM, i.e. $t_i \leq \mu_2$

The dependent variable y denotes three sets of observed technologies, which are grouped in order of increasing sophistication described above. The latent variable, t_i is assumed to be the unobserved intensity of IT use, while X_i denotes a vector of firm-specific characteristics that may influence the probability of using more sophisticated technologies. t_i, determines the use of a more sophisticated group of technologies for the *i*th trucking firm. The vector X_i contains the time sensitivity of the route, route variability, average load, average haul, total equipment, debt-to-equity ratio, net profit margin, and the sum of up to five additional information-processing (complementary) technologies. The cumulative distribution of ε is assumed to be normal. The unobserved index t_i

is assumed to have two thresholds, μ_1 and μ_2. Crossing each threshold is associated with a transition to using a new set of technologies. Maximum likelihood estimates of μ and β are obtained to investigate the impact of haul characteristics on IT use.

4. DATA

Empirical evidence about the influence of a firm's objectives on IT use is scarce, because this type of data is rarely collected. Recently, a data set containing detailed information on marketing objectives as well as IT use has become available. This data set is the Motor Carrier Safety, Operations, and Technology (MCSOT) Survey, conducted by the American Trucking Association (ATA). The survey contains a special module in which respondents report the use of various types of information-gathering and information-processing (complementary) technologies. In addition to being the unique source of detailed IT data, the survey contains other information (e.g. a firm's ranking of marketing objectives and operational characteristics) relevant to testing the hypothesis outlined above. The survey information used below was collected in June 1998, and the data for technology use cover both 1996 and 1998.

Our empirical investigation also uses data drawn from a second source, the U.S. Department of Transportation's Bureau of Transportation Statistics (DOT). The bureau queries 2,800 class 1 and class 2 for-hire trucking firms (≥ $3 million revenue) that are engaged in interstate commerce.[7] Owing to non-responses, the final 1996 survey contains information on 1,800 firms. The DOT data contains the name of each firm as well as other detailed information (e.g. full income statement, balance sheet, labor force information, equipment data, and operating statistics). These data (specific variables described below) provide control variables for our empirical model.[8]

The ATA's MCSOT survey was sent to the 1,800 firms contained in the DOT data, and 755 of these responded. Ignoring missing values ($n = 26$), extreme values for firm size ($n = 8$), and firms that report owning no trucks ($n = 18$) leaves our final merged data sample at 703 firms.

Variable Descriptions and Expected Coefficients

A. Marketing Objectives and Commodities Hauled

Table 1 describes the firms' primary marketing objectives according to the industry's conventional organizational structure: truckload (TL) and less-than-truckload (LTL).[9] Briefly stated, TL carriers are point-to-point operators – single trucks hauling their load directly from origin to destination – typically

Table 1. Distribution of Primary Marketing Objectives.

Firm's Primary Marketing Objective	Organizational Structure of the Market			
	All Firms (Censored)*	Only TL	Only LTL	Specialized
On-Time Performance	439 (71.85%)	184 (77.31%)	45 (84.91%)	210 (77.19%)
Lowest Freight Rate	61 (9.98%)	18 (7.56%)	6 (11.32%)	37 (11.56%)
Safety	32 (5.24%)	12 (5.04%)	0	20 (14.06)
Specialized/Dedicated Equipment	66 (10.80%)	19 (7.98%)	2 (3.77%)	45 (3.77%)
Short Turn-Around on Customers Request	13 (2.13%)	5 (2.10%)	0	8 (2.50)
Non-On-Time Performance (Rows 4 through 7)	172 (28.15%)	54 (22.69%)	8 (15.09%)	110 (22.91%)
Sample Size	611	238	53	320

* The entire sample (all firms uncensored) is 703 firms. The censored sample of 611 (column 2) excludes 92 firms that listed more than one primary marketing objective.

carrying more than 10,000 pounds. LTL carriers use an airline-type hub-and-spoke system with shipments of less than 10,000 pounds.[10] The table shows the vast majority of firms (72%) market themselves as on-time performers (OTP). Eighty-five percent of the LTL firms are OTP while only 77% of the TL firms are OTP.

Table 2 describes the percentage of firms that haul each commodity.[11] The patterns of this table seem reasonable. More firms haul goods that are normally associated with timely deliveries and whose primary marketing objective is on-time performance versus non-on-time performance. For example, parcels, processed food, and retail goods are hauled by more on-time performers than non-on-time performers (see columns 3 and 4). On the other hand, more non-on-time performers haul nonperishable goods, such as dump-trucking and mineral ores. More firms whose objective is to provide specialized and dedicated equipment (see column 7) haul hazardous chemicals and heavy machinery. A notable overall pattern is that various firms represented by varying marketing

Table 2. Percentage of Firms Hauling Each Commodity.

Goods Hauled	Firm's Primary Marketing Objective						
	All Firms*	On-Time Performers	Non-On-Time Performers (Cols. 4–7)	Lowest Freight Rate	Safety	Specialized Equipment	Short Turnaround
Auto Parts or Vehicles	0.16	0.16	0.12	0.08	0.19	0.11	0.23
Raw Petroleum Products	0.04	0.03	0.08	0.11	0.03	0.06	0.08
Mine Ores	0.03	0.02	0.05	0.03	0.09	0.06	0.00
Processed Food	0.24	0.27	0.17	0.18	0.09	0.17	0.31
Parcels	0.05	0.06	0.01	0.02	0.00	0.02	0.00
Heavy Machinery	0.15	0.13	0.19	0.13	0.25	0.23	0.15
Refined Petroleum Products	0.11	0.10	0.13	0.13	0.03	0.17	0.15
Forest Products	0.15	0.15	0.18	0.11	0.09	0.29	0.15
Farm-Fresh Products	0.14	0.14	0.12	0.15	0.06	0.14	0.08
Refuse	0.02	0.02	0.005	0.00	0.00	0.00	0.08
Household Goods	0.06	0.05	0.06	0.10	0.03	0.05	0.00
Dump Trucking	0.10	0.07	0.17	0.16	0.13	0.20	0.23
Retail	0.14	0.15	0.10	0.11	0.09	0.12	0.00
Building Materials	0.24	0.23	0.26	0.21	0.28	0.32	0.15
Hazardous Chemicals	0.15	0.15	0.19	0.20	0.06	0.27	0.08
Sample Size	703	439	172	61	32	66	13

Notes: The percentages for each column do not add to 100% because most trucking firms haul more than one commodity.

* The entire sample (column 2 – all firms *un*censored) is 703 firms. The censored sample (columns 3 plus 4) of 611 excludes 92 firms that listed more than one primary marketing objective.

objectives haul virtually all products. For example, 13% of on-time performers haul heavy machinery while 13% of firms offering the lowest freight rate also haul heavy machinery.

B. Technologies

Our empirical specification emphasizes the distinction between information-gathering and information-processing (complementary) technologies. Following Hubbard (1998), we say that an information-gathering technology is one that resides on the truck. The question we examine – what determines technology use – refers to information-gathering technologies. For example, we categorize satellite communications as a gathering technology. One of its functions is to provide the driver and dispatchers information about the location of the truck. An example of a technology that processes information is computer-aided dispatching. Sometimes a gathering technology cannot be used without a processing technology, whereas in other cases, they can be used independently.

We acknowledge that there are many gray areas in categorizing these technologies, and that it is difficult to create clear partitions. We assume the following reasonable, intuitive categories. The information-gathering technologies used to create our dependent variable are cell phones, two-way radios, and pagers (low technology), and AVL systems, satellite communications, and on-board computers (high technology). The information-processing technologies are electronic data interchange, computer-aided routing, computer-aided dispatching, the Internet, and maintenance-tracking software. We use the information-gathering technologies to construct our limited dependent variable describing technology use. The sum of the five processing technologies is used as a control variable.[12]

Table 3 contains descriptive statistics for the use of each technology. The incidence of technology use is as expected. Among the gathering technologies for all firms (column 2), the low technologies – cell phones and pagers – are used by the largest percentage of the firms, 61% and 56% respectively. Fewer firms (AVL systems [23%], satellite communications [32%], and on-board computers [7%]) use the more sophisticated and more expensive gathering technologies (high technologies). Two-way radios are both low-technology and inexpensive, yet are used by a relatively small percentage of firms (31%). Perhaps the usefulness of two-way radios in improving productivity has been overshadowed by cell phones and pagers. Finally, it seems reasonable that very few firms (5%) use no technology at all.

Reasonable patterns of technology use emerge by comparing on-time performers (OTPs, column 3) with firms offering the lowest freight rate (LFR – column 4), and with all firms that are *non*-OTP. The sophisticated technologies (e.g. automatic vehicle location systems) are used by more OTP firms (compared to LFR or *non*-OTP) whereas the low technologies (e.g. cell phones) are used by more LFR and *non*-OTP firms (than by OTP firms.) The OTP firms also use more information-processing technologies (e.g. computer-aided routing

Table 3. Sample Means of Technology Use.

Information Technology Use	Firm's Primary Marketing Objective			
	All Firms*	On-Time Performers	Lowest Freight Rate	Non-On-Time Performers
Low Technology – Information Gathering				
Cell phone 1998	0.61	0.60	0.69	0.67
Pager 1998	0.56	0.52	0.64	0.66
Two-way Radio 1998	0.31	0.31	0.43	0.34
High Technology – Information Gathering				
Auto Vehicle Location 1998	0.23	0.25	0.10	0.20
On-Board Computers 1998	0.07	0.07	0.03	0.06
Satellite Comm. 1998	0.32	0.32	0.21	0.30
Information Processing				
Computer-Aided Dispatching 1996	0.29	0.31	0.18	0.28
Computer-Aided Routing 1996	0.22	0.23	0.15	0.24
Electronic Data Interchange 1996	0.29	0.32	0.26	0.28
Internet 1996	0.10	0.10	0.08	0.09
Maintenance Tracking Software 1996	0.17	0.19	0.15	0.16
Others				
No IT use	0.05	0.06	0.08	0.03
No Info Gathering Technology 1998	0.11	0.13	0.11	0.08
No Info Processing Technology 1996	0.47	0.45	0.59	0.45
Sample Size	703	439	61	172

* The entire sample (column 2 – all firms uncensored) is 703 firms. The censored sample (columns 3 plus 5) of 611 excludes 92 firms that listed more than one primary marketing objective.

and dispatching) than their LFR counterparts. It seems that the OTP firms use the higher technologies to meet their marketing objective, even though these technologies are generally more expensive.

C. Explanatory Variables

The empirical model described above contains a vector of control variables X_i that are assumed to influence the probability of using more highly sophisticated information-gathering technologies. Table 4 contains sample means of these variables.

Table 4. Sample Means of Explanatory Variables.

Firm Characteristics	Most Important Marketing Objective			
	All Firms*	On-Time Performers	Lowest Freight Rate	Non-On-Time Performers
Time-Sensitive Hauls (Scale: 1–5)	3.90	3.98	3.85	3.80
Route Variability (Scale: 1–4)	3.20	3.15	3.28	3.29
Average Load (Tons)	14.93	14.64	15.26	16.52
Average Haul (Miles)	554.06	521.64	751.15	637.42
Total Equipment (Power Units and Trailers)	414.48	437.55	260.85	356.12
Leverage (Debt/Equity)	0.56	0.57	0.49	0.53
Net Profit Margin (Net Income/Gross Rev.)	1.58	1.59	1.32	1.83
Information Processing Technology (Scale: 0-5)	1.08	1.15	0.82	1.04
Sample Size	703	439	61	172

* The entire sample (column 2 – all firms uncensored) is 703 firms. The censored sample (columns 3 plus 5) of 611 excludes 92 firms that listed more than one primary marketing objective.

One of our two key explanatory variables describes the percentage of the firm's dispatches that are time sensitive or perishable (row 1). The variable ranges from 1 to 5, 1 indicating that none of the dispatches is time sensitive, 2 indicating that 1 to 25% are time sensitive, etc. The 3.9 average for time sensitivity in Table 4 indicates that for the average firm, between 26 and 50% of their dispatches are time sensitive. As expected, those firms that market themselves as on-time performers haul more time-sensitive goods than do non-on-time performers. We expect that the probability of using more sophisticated technology will increase as the proportion of time-sensitive hauls increases *if the firm markets itself as an on-time performer.*

Our second key explanatory variable describes the variability of the company's routes (row 2). It ranges from 1 to 4, 1 indicating not at all variable, and 4 indicating extremely variable. The probability of using sophisticated technology should rise as the route variability rises, *only with firms for which the variability of the route may preclude them from obtaining their objective.* For example, an on-time performer that hauls mostly within the hub-and-spoke system (LTL hauler) should be expected to use more sophisticated technology in response to an increase in route variability. In contrast, a point-to-point hauler (TL hauler) is not expected to use high-technology gadgets in response to more variable routes. TL haulers' objectives are different. The incentive to use information-gathering technology should, then, be clearly related to how the production activity is organized.

Both time sensitivity and route variability are firm-specific haul characteristics. We expect that these characteristics will influence the use of IT differently, depending on how firms market themselves to their customers. Our data include a variable that ranks each firm's marketing objectives among five items – providing the lowest freight rates, on-time performance, short turnaround, safety of performance, and availability of specialized equipment. We assume that if a firm ranks on-time performance as its most important marketing objective, then being on time is a key component of that firm's output. With this in mind, we run separate regressions on firms with different marketing objectives.

Grimm et al. (1989), McMullen (1987), and McMullen and Tanaka (1995) explain costs in the motor carrier industry and include output attributes as explanatory variables to help capture the heterogeneity of output. Our investigation of IT use has the same concern – to reduce heterogeneity in our sample as much as possible – so that the impact of marketing objectives can be more clearly examined. The output attributes we include to reduce heterogeneity are the average load and the average haul. The average load indicates the number of tons transported by each unit dispatched. The average haul length measures how far the average unit travels each time it is dispatched.

A low average load indicates that the trucks operate more frequently, reflecting higher quality service. Trucks with lighter loads are more often LTL carriers where operating costs are typically higher for many reasons. Coupled with the need for more advanced hub-and-spoke infrastructure, an LTL carrier should find more sophisticated technology useful for coordination purposes (Hubbard, 1998). We expect that trucks with a smaller average load will use more sophisticated technology – a negative coefficient on average load.

A longer average haul length indicates the need for more sophisticated technology, such as satellite communications and automatic vehicle location systems. The further the truck is from home, the less cost-effective is a cell phone or a pager. We expect a positive coefficient on average haul. Columns 3 and 4 in Table 4 reveal that on-time performers have a lower average load and a lower average haul than their counterparts that offer the lowest freight rate. This makes sense, since absent the need to be on time, firms offering the lowest freight rate concentrate on reducing average costs by making sure their trucks are fuller (higher average load) and travel longer distances (higher average haul).

Total equipment is defined as the number of trucks plus tractors plus trailers. This variable controls for the size of the firm's operation. On-time performers operate more units than LFR firms (Table 4). Firms offering the lowest freight rate as their specialty do not need the larger fleets to ensure on-time delivery. We also include the net profit margin (net income as a percent of gross revenue) as a control variable to ensure that our results are not driven by the firm's financial well-being.

Zingales (1998) explains the survival of post-deregulation trucking firms with the level of pre-deregulation leverage. He finds that highly leveraged firms are less likely to survive. We include the debt-to-equity ratio to control for the firm's leverage and are uncertain about this variable's coefficient. More highly leveraged firms may be indicative of the ability to borrow to acquire sophisticated IT, but it may also indicate that the firm has already exhausted its borrowing capacity. If the firm is unable to borrow, it is less capable of adopting sophisticated technology.

5. RESULTS

Main Findings

Our estimation strategy investigates the impact of haul characteristics on the use of information technology. The question to be examined is: Does the impact of haul characteristics on IT use vary depending upon the firm's marketing strategy? If the answer is yes, then two firms may seem to offer identical services yet in fact offer different services as a result of disparate marketing strategies and varying IT usage. Outputs might then be grouped incorrectly in productivity studies, and the impact of IT on productivity may be mismeasured.

We investigate the variation in IT use with two separate specifications. In the first specification, we categorize information-gathering technologies used on the truck as either high-tech or low-tech. These two groups serve to define our dependent variable for probit estimates (Table 5). In our second specification, we create three groups of IT use, in order of increasing sophistication. These ordered probit estimates are presented in tables 6 and 7. A list of variable means for all explanatory variables is presented in Table 4. Table 5, specification 1 predicts the use of IT for the entire sample ($n = 703$). Specifications 2 and 3 partition the sample according to whether or not the firm's primary marketing objective is to be an on-time performer.[13]

Table 5. Probit Estimates – Impact of Haul Characteristics on IT Use.

Variable	Estimated Coefficient (Standard Error)		
	All Firms[a]	On-Time Performers	Non-On-Time Performers
Time-Sensitive Hauls	0.082	0.125	−0.003
	(0.042)**	(0.056)**	(0.083)
Route Variability	0.083	0.175	−0.130
	(0.068)	(0.089)**	(0.142)
Average Load	−0.0174	−0.021	−0.0007
(Tons)	(0.0071)**	(0.0100)**	(0.0136)
Average Haul	0.0002	0.0003	0.0005
(Miles)	(0.0001)**	(0.0001)**	(0.0002)**
Total Equipment (Power Units and Trailers)	0.0002	0.0001	0.00122
	(0.00006)***	(0.00006)*	(0.00031)***
Leverage (Debt/Equity)	0.750	0.818	0.023
	(0.208)***	(0.260)***	(0.455)
Net Profit Margin (Net Income/Gross Rev.)	0.020	0.022	0.001
	(0.013)	(0.017)	(0.025)
Information-Processing	0.203	0.201	0.252
Technology (Scale: 0-5)	(0.040)***	(0.049)***	(0.091)***
Log Likelihood	−416.23	−260.84	−86.56
Dependent Variable Mean	0.36	0.36	0.47
Sample Size	703	439	172

Notes: Dependent variable is 1 if the firm uses Satellite Communication or On-board Computers or Automated Vehicle Locators. Dependent variable is zero otherwise. *, ** and *** indicate 90%, 95%, and 99% level of significance, respectively.

[a] The entire sample (column 2 – all firms uncensored) is 703 firms. The censored sample (columns 3 plus 4) of 611 excludes 92 firms that listed more than one primary marketing objective.

The evidence indicates that a firm's use of increasingly sophisticated IT varies considerably depending on its marketing strategy. For those firms that market themselves as on-time performers (Table 5, specification 2), the estimated probit coefficients are positive and significant at the five-percent level for both the proportion of time-sensitive hauls and for the firm's route variability. For firms with marketing objectives *other than* on-time performance, the coefficients for those same key haul characteristics are statistically insignificant (specification 3).

For on-time performers (specification 2) at sample means, a 25% rise in the number of time-sensitive hauls increases the probability of using sophisticated

IT by 5%. For non-on-time performers, the same 25% rise in time-sensitive hauls has a statistically insignificant impact on technology use. The impact of time-sensitive hauls on technology use is 50% higher for on-time performers compared to the entire sample.

The impact of route variability on the use of information-gathering technology follows the same pattern as the impact of time-sensitive hauls. On-time performers use more sophisticated technology as routes become more variable, while for non-on-time performers route variability has no impact. For on-time performers, a 25% rise in route variability increases the probability of using sophisticated technology by 7%. The impact of route variability on technology use is 100% higher for on-time performers compared to the entire sample.

The sharp difference between the estimates for on-time performers versus non-on-time performers supports the hypothesis that a firm's measured output must incorporate information about service-oriented, firm-specific goals. Productivity studies that aggregate overall firms producing the same physical good are likely to misrepresent the true output of the firm. Firms with different customer-oriented goals (e.g. on-time performers vs. non-on-time performers) use different technologies in response to variations in the *same haul characteristics*. The services and, therefore, the output that the on-time performer produces are clearly different.

The remaining estimates in Table 5 for on-time performers (specification 2) accord with several of our predictions outlined in the data section above. A notable result indicated by the log likelihood is that the combined explanatory variables perform better at explaining technology use within a particular marketing objective (on-time performers) than for the sample that includes all other marketing objectives combined (non-on-time performers).

To reduce sample heterogeneity, we included average load and average haul as output attributes. Trucks with a smaller average load use more sophisticated IT, possibly owing to the need for more coordination. The significantly positive impact of average haul indicates that trucks traveling longer distances are more likely to use sophisticated IT.

The total equipment coefficient suggests that larger operations find the more sophisticated technologies useful, perhaps again for coordination purposes. Yet the insignificant coefficient on net profit margin raises doubts about firms buying IT simply because they have the cash.

Firms use significantly higher levels of information technology as they become more leveraged. It may be that they are borrowing to acquire some of the more expensive technologies, such as satellite communications. Finally, it makes sense that firms with more highly sophisticated gathering technologies will be more likely to have more processing (complementary) technologies.

Additional Findings

We address possible objections to our above specification by splitting our sample in a more traditional manner (TL and LTL), and by using an alternate (ordered) categorization of the technologies contained in the dependent variable. Our additional findings indicate that our main results are robust.

One alternative for creating our dependent variable is to use a categorization of technologies that reflects an order of sophistication, which includes no technologies, some low-level gadgets, and highly sophisticated gadgets. Grouping together firms that use no technologies with those using low-level yet highly effective technologies, such as cell phones, may raise questions regarding the validity of our result. To address this potential concern, we reestimate the Table 5 specifications using the ordered probit model described in the empirical specification section above. Our results, presented in Table 6, still indicate that firms choose more sophisticated technologies differently depending on their marketing objective.

Second, our results may be questioned since we neglect to control for the highly heterogeneous organizational structure in the motor carrier industry. As mentioned earlier, TL and LTL carriers operate differently along many dimensions. We partition our sample along the TL/LTL lines, yet we find that this categorization is not the main concern when estimating IT use. Specifications 1 and 2 in Table 7 indicate that for all firms, neither time sensitivity nor route variability has a statistically significant impact on technology use. This split does little to resolve the problem that occurs owing to aggregating over heterogeneous competitive strategies.[14]

Specifications 3, 4, and 5 in Table 7 support our previous conclusion: the important categorization in explaining variation in IT use is the firm's primary objective for quality customer service. There is a notable difference in results between TL and LTL firms for on-time performers. Specification 4 (LTL firms only) reveals that route variability has a significantly positive influence on IT adoption. This statistically significant effect is not present for only TL firms (specification 3). For on-time performers, the time-sensitivity of hauls has a statistically significant positive impact on technology use. This result holds for both TL and LTL firms (specifications 3 and 4). For TL firms that are not concerned with on-time performance (specification 5), these haul characteristics have no impact.[15] A notable difference in results between TL and LTL firms for on-time performers is that the route-variability coefficient is much larger for the LTL firms. Firms in both categories may have equivalently variable routes, yet associate different uncertainties with that variation. The uncertainty is likely to be higher for the LTL firms, and therefore, the more sophisticated technology would be more useful for them.

Table 6. Ordered Probit Estimates – Impact of Haul Characteristics on IT Use.

Variable	Estimated Coefficient (Standard Error)		
	All Firms[a]	On-Time Performers	Non-On-Time Performers
Time-Sensitive Hauls	0.059	0.109	−0.035
	(0.035)*	(0.047)**	(0.070)
Route Variability	0.043	0.064	−0.015
	(0.057)	(0.074)	(0.120)
Average Load	−0.014	−0.0184	0.0032
	(0.0059)**	(0.0082)**	(0.0111)
Average Haul	0.0001	0.0002	0.0002
Total Equipment	0.00019	0.00009	0.00126
(Power Units and Trailers)	(0.00006)***	(0.00006)	(0.0003)***
Leverage (Debt/Equity)	0.584	0.631	0.086
	(0.178)***	(0.223)***	(0.383)
Net Profit Margin			
(Net Income/Gross Rev.)	0.020	0.022	0.005
	(0.011)	(0.014)	(0.020)
Information-Processing	0.164	0.161	0.216
Technology (Scale: 0–5)	(0.036)***	(0.044)***	(0.082)***
Cut 1[b]	−0.444	−0.134	−0.907
	(0.273)*	(0.352)	(0.565)
Cut 2[b]	1.219	1.430	1.181
	(0.275)***	(0.356)***	(0.568)**
Log Likelihood	−634.17	−407.17	−130.09
Sample Size	703	439	172

Notes: Dependent variable is 1 if the firm does not use any information-gathering technologies. Dependent variable is 2 if the firm only uses low technologies – cell phones, pagers, or two-way radios. Dependent variable is 3 if the firm uses high technologies – Satellite Communications, on-board computers, or Automated Vehicle Locators. Dependent variable is zero otherwise. *, ** and *** indicate 90%, 95%, and 99% level of significance, respectively.

[a] The entire sample (column 2 – all firms uncensored) is 703 firms. The censored sample (columns 3 plus 4) of 611 excludes 92 firms that listed more than one primary marketing objective.

[b] The estimated thresholds (Cut 1 and Cut 2) are significantly different from each other at 99% level of significance.

Table 7. Ordered Probit Estimates – Impact of Haul Characteristics on IT Use by Marketing Objectives and Industry Structure.

Variable	Estimated Coefficients				
	All Firms[a]		On-Time Performers		Non-On-Time Performers
	TL	LTL	TL	LTL	TL
Time-Sensitive Hauls	0.072	0.192	0.131	0.457	−0.123
	(0.062)	(0.165)	(0.075)*	(0.232)***	(0.162)
Route Variability	−0.069	0.239	0.021	0.497	−0.355
	(0.099)	(0.205)	(0.122)	(0.257)*	(0.239)
Average Load	−0.0063	0.0289	−0.0167	0.0346	0.0359
	(0.0102)	(0.0361)	(0.0127)	(0.0412)	(0.0258)
Average Haul	0.0003	−0.0003	0.0004	−0.0001	0.0005
	(0.0001)**	(0.0007)	(0.0002)**	(0.0009)	(0.0003)
Total Equipment (Power Units and Trailers)	0.00051	0.00002	0.00037	-0.00005	0.00181
	(0.00015)***	(0.00010)	(0.00017)**	(0.00011)	(0.00075)**
Leverage (Debt/Equity)	0.349	1.071	0.437	1.282	−0.118
	(0.302)	(0.811)	(0.356)	(0.978)	(0.716)
Net Profit Margin (Net Income/Gross Rev.)	0.007	0.013	0.007	0.039	0.009
	(0.018)	(0.063)	(0.025)	(0.070)	(0.034)
Information-Processing Technology (Scale: 0-5)	0.141	0.243	0.146	0.311	0.053
	(0.057)**	(0.141)*	(0.065)**	(0.171)*	(0.162)
Cut 1[b]	−0.461	0.372	0.071	2.396	−1.521
	(0.474)	(0.966)	(0.553)	(1.344)*	(1.280)
Cut 2[b]	0.972	3.125	1.452	5.239	0.086
	(0.475)**	(1.056)***	(0.559)***	(1.566)***	(1.262)
Log Likelihood	−245.55	−38.21	−173.92	−27.97	−45.06
Sample Size	266	59	184	45	54

Notes: Dependent variable is 1 if the firm does not use any information-gathering technologies. Dependent variable is 2 if the firm only uses low technologies – cell phones, pagers, or two-way radios. Dependent variable is 3 if the firm uses high technologies – satellite communications, on-board computers, or Automated Vehicle Locators. Dependent variable is zero otherwise. *, ** and *** indicate 90%, 95%, and 99% level of significance, respectively. We cannot compare LTL on-time performers with LTL non-on-time performers since the sample size for LTL non-on-time performers is only 8.

[a] All firms (columns 2 plus 3 – 325 firms) excludes specialized carriers. The censored sample (columns 4 through 6 – 283 firms) also excludes firms that listed more than one primary marketing objective.

[b] The estimated thresholds (Cut 1 and Cut 2) are significantly different from each other at 99% level of significance.

6. CONCLUSION

The estimates presented above indicate that marketing objectives are a pivotal factor in determining the use of information technology. We find that sophisticated IT is used differently by firms with similar haul characteristics yet different marketing strategies. Firms that market themselves as on-time performers use IT differently than do firms that have other marketing criteria. This finding is important because marketing strategies can add distinct quality dimensions to a good or service. Previous research has found that a primary reason for the productivity paradox is the incorrect measuring of outputs. Our results indicate that output cannot be measured correctly until the impact of marketing objectives – the quality dimension of the good – is recognized. Even in firm-level productivity studies, precise measurement of the influence of IT on productivity should control for the quality dimension of the good. One way to accomplish this might be to group firms producing similar goods and services according to their primary marketing objectives.

NOTES

1. Brynjolfsson (1993) and Wilson (1993) survey the literature that investigates the impact of information technology on productivity.
2. The probit model simply collapses the first two categories of the ordered probit into one category.
3. The haul characteristics in our model include the time-sensitivity of the goods, and the route variability of the haul.
4. Please see the variable descriptions and expected coefficients in the data section below for a detailed explanation of the distinction.
5. Incentive benefits can help firms align workers' pay with their productivity.
6. Please see the data section and the appendix below for a detailed description of technologies.
7. For-hire trucks are those that are not part of a private fleet. For example the hypothetical firm Acme Retailers employs a for-hire trucking company to deliver goods to its retail outlets – Acme doesn't maintain its own private fleet.
8. Both the Transportation Technical Services Company (Blue Book database) and the ATA (Financial and Operating Statistics) organize and summarize the DOT data into machine-readable form. We use variables from both sources.
9. Our entire sample (*un*censored) includes 703 firms. Only 611 firms (Table 1, column 2 – all firms censored) could unambiguously categorize their marketing objective.
10. For a more detailed description of these categorizations, see Swan (1997).
11. Since each firm might haul many different products, the columns do not add to 100.
12. Hubbard (1998) emphasizes the importance of processing technologies in explaining the use of information-gathering technology. He labels the processing technologies "backoffice" technologies. His data does not contain information on these

backoffice technologies, and he takes special care to empirically confirm that his model has no bias owing to the exclusion of this type of technology.

13. The number of observations for on-time performers (439) plus non-on-time performers (172) does not sum to 703 because we dropped 92 firms that reported more than one primary marketing objective.

14. In Table 7, all firms (columns 2 plus 3–325 firms) excludes specialized carriers. The censored sample (columns 4 through 6–283 firms) also excludes firms that listed more than one primary marketing objective.

15. We cannot compare LTL on-time performers with LTL non-on-time performers since the sample size for LTL non-on-time performers is only 8.

16. We wish to thank Bob Pritchard for his contribution to this appendix. Parts of this appendix draws heavily and reproduces portions of information exactly from Commercial Vehicle Fleet Management and Information Systems, Technical Memorandum 3, ITS Fleet Management Technology Resource Guide, prepared by Cambridge Systematics, Inc., in cooperation with ATA Foundation Private Fleet Management Institute. The memorandum was prepared for the Federal Highway Administration, May 1996.

ACKNOWLEDGMENTS

We wish to thank Richard Arnott, Kit Baum, Ernie Berndt, Ellie Berman, Eric Brynjolfsson, Russ Campbell, Don Cox, Robert J. Gordon, Thomas Hubbard, Adam Jaffe, Bob Pritchard, Matthew D. Shapiro, Kathryn L. Shaw, Dan Stock, Dan Swaine, seminar participants at the NBER productivity workshop, and the Federal Reserve Bank of Boston for many helpful comments. We also thank seminar participants from the Northeast Transportation Institute's third annual conference at Atlantic City. Research assistance was provided by Andy Simms. This research was funded by the NBER through a grant from the Alfred P. Sloan Foundation. We also thank the American Trucking Association for providing the data, and James Coyne and Judy Feldmann for copyediting the paper.

REFERENCES

Brynjolfsson, E. (December, 1993). The Productivity Paradox of Information Technology. *Communications of the ACM*, *35*, 66–77.

Brynjolfsson, E., & Hitt, L. (1998). Beyond the Productivity Paradox. *Communication of the ACM*, *41*(8), 49–55.

Brynjolfsson, E. (1996). Paradox Lost? Firm-Level Evidence on the Returns to Information Systems Spending. *Management Science*, *42*(4), 541–558.

Brynjolfsson, E. (1995). Information Technology as a Factor of Production: The Role of Differences among Firms. *Economic Innovation and New Technology*, *3*, 183–199.

Dewan, S., & Min, C.-K. (1997). The Substitution of Information Technology for Other Factors of Production: A Firm Level Analysis. *Management Science*, *43*(2), 1660–1675.

Dos Santos, B. L., Peffers, K. G., & Mauer, D. C. (1993). The Impact of Information Technology Investment Announcements on the Market Value of the Firm. *Information Systems Res.*, *4*(1), 1–23.

Grimm, C. M., Corsi, T. M., & Jarrell, J. L. (Fall, 1989). U.S. Motor Carrier Cost Structure Under Deregulation. *Logistics and Transportation Review*, *25*(3), 231–249.

Hubbard, T. (August 4, 1998). *Why Are Monitoring Technologies Valuable? The Use of On-Board Information Technology in the Trucking Industry*. UCLA and NBER, Mimeo.

Lichtenberg, R. (May, 1995). The Output Contributions of Computer Equipment and Personnel: A Firm-Level Analysis. *Economics of Innovation and New Technology*, *3*(3–4), 201–217.

Loveman, G. W. (1994). An Assessment of the Productivity Impact on Information Technologies, In: T. J. Allen & M. S. S. Morton (Eds), *Information Technology and the Corporation of the 1990s: Research Studies*. Cambridge, MA: MIT Press.

McMullen, B. S. (September, 1987). The Impact of Regulatory Reform on U.S. Motor Carrier Costs. *Journal of Transport Economics and Policy*, 307–318.

McMullen, B. S., & Tanaka, H. (1995). An Econometric Analysis of Differences Between Motor Carriers: Implications for Market Structure. *Quarterly Journal of Business and Economics*, *34*(4), 16–29.

Morrison, C. J., & Berndt, E. R. (January, 1990). Assessing the Productivity of Information Technology Equipment in the U.S. Manufacturing Industries, NBER Working Paper 3582.

Porter, M. E. (1985a). Technology and Competitive Advantage. *Journal of Business Strategy*, *5*, 60–68.

Porter, M. E. (1985b). *Competitive Advantage: Creating and Sustaining Superior Performance*. The Free Press.

Porter, M. E., & Millar, V. E. (July – August, 1985c). How Information Gives You a Competitive Advantage. *Harvard Business Review*, 149–160.

Roach, S. S. (April, 1987). *America's Technology Dilemma: A Profile of the Information Economy*. Morgan Stanley Special Economic Study.

Siegel, D., & Griliches, Z. (April, 1991). Purchased Services, Outsourcing, Computers, and Productivity in Manufacturing. NBER Working Paper 3678.

Solow, R. (July 12, 1987). *New York Times Book Review*.

Swan, P. F. (1997). The Effect of Changes in Operations on Less-Than-Truckload Motor Carrier Productivity and Survival. Ph.D. Dissertation, The University of Michigan.

Wilson, D. (1993). Assessing the Impact of Information Technology on Organizational Performance, In: R. Barker, R. Kauffman & M. A. Mahmood (Eds), *Strategic Information Technology Management*. Idea Group, Harrisburg, PA.

Zingales, L. (1998). Survival of the Fittest or the Fattest? Exit and Financing in the Trucking Industry. *The Journal of Finance*, *3*(3), 905–938.

APPENDIX – DESCRIPTION OF TECHNOLOGIES

This appendix provides brief descriptions of each of the eleven technologies listed in the paper. These technologies are used for fleet management, and to enhance the competitive advantage of the industry and of individual trucking companies by improving the efficiency of goods movements through real-time information exchange and communications, and by providing customers with up-to-the-minute information regarding the location and timing of shipments and deliveries.

Low-Technology Communications and Information Gathering

1. Cellular phones
These mobile communication devices transmit voice and data. While this technology is common, service areas are limited and dead zones exist in less-populated areas, mountainous areas, tunnels, or anywhere transmitters are sparse.

2. Two-Way Radios
Voice conversations are transmitted via these proprietary radio systems. The ranges of two-way radios can extent to 50 miles with the appropriate transmitter.

3. Pagers
One-way text messages are transmitted to a small receiver via a number of paging networks. The range is only constrained by the type of supporting technology.

High Technology for Information Gathering

4, 5. Automatic Vehicle Location (AVL), and Satellite Communications (SATCOM)
AVL is a broad descriptive category of technologies to track the location of transponders. It is possible to pinpoint the location of a vehicle using ground-based or satellite technologies. When combined with on-board computers and routing and dispatching software, these systems allow for real-time optimization of fleet routing and dispatching. Drivers, dispatchers, shippers, and receivers can track a truck from pickup to delivery, perform just-in-time deliveries, coordinate intermodal shipments, and provide improved customer service. Satellite communications provide AVL capabilities and also communications between the vehicle and dispatcher. With an on-board computer, two-way text

or voice communications can allow for dynamic routing and dispatching, as well as the real-time monitoring of vehicle operating parameters (speed, RPMs, etc.). Satellite systems are less effective in urban areas because their radio-navigation signals are reflected and distorted by buildings, bridges, power lines, and other structures. Ground-based AVL are more reliable in urban areas, which may make this technology more attractive to short-haul motor carriers. Since sufficient antenna coverage for ground-based systems does not exist throughout the U.S., satellite systems that have global coverage can be used more effectively by long-haul carriers.

6. On-Board Computers (OBCs)

OBCs are either vehicle-based or handheld computers used to capture information from the vehicle or by the driver. OBCs are sometimes used as trip recorders, for monitoring vehicle performance measures such as speed, fuel consumption, and drivers' hours of service. Information stored in OBCs can be uploaded to the dispatch center using mobile communication systems or downloaded to a system when the truck returns to its domicile. OBCs are often used as a platform for two-way text communications and sometimes in conjunction with routing and dispatching systems as well as with maintenance-scheduling software. OBCs can provide the following functions:

- Business Transactions: Registers delivery times, state line crossings, and customer signatures for proof-of-delivery; transmits delivery notifications.
- Driver Log: Enables drivers to input records of fuel consumption and hours of service using a keyboard and display screen.
- Vehicle Location Information: Deciphers AVL system transmissions.
- Vehicle performance data collection: Engine idling, braking, shifting, and acceleration patterns, as well as data from diagnostic systems for ancillary equipment such as refrigeration units can be captured. OBCs can allow for remote diagnostics prior to a malfunction in order to improve the safety performance of vehicles.

Technology for Information Processing

7. Electronic Data Interchange (EDI)

A series of standardized messages constitutes the umbrella concept of EDI and allows for computer-to-computer data transmission. The transmissions can occur between trucking companies and shippers, or between any two trading partners. EDI allows for automatic scheduling, billing, receipt of load acknowledgment, etc.

8, 9. Computer-Aided Routing, and Dispatching (CAR and CAD)

Routing and dispatching software provides decision support for route selection in order to minimize the time and cost of moving freight. Systems are used to schedule trucks and drivers subject to availability of parameters, such as allowable driving hours, size of load, origin, and destination. Static systems allow for preplanning. More sophisticated dynamic systems allow routing and dispatch decisions based on real-time truck locations, generate route maps, estimate delivery times and distances, and help improve cost estimates. These software systems provide the following benefits:

- Improved dispatcher productivity: Companies report that routing procedures, which previously took staff eight hours with a manual system, now can be finished in one hour.
- Reduced client inventory costs: With the reliable delivery provided by CAR and CAD systems, just-in-time inventory systems can be more commonly used and manufacture on demand is also made feasible. With these software systems, firms no longer need to keep extensive inventories at manufacturing plants.
- Improved communication efficiency: With a computerized system, load information to drivers can be relayed instantaneously.
- Reduced labor costs: Companies do not need to employ logistics experts to operate these systems. Simple user interfaces make it possible for employees without specialized training to operate the system. Shippers can make their routing and dispatching information available on the Internet so that receivers can track shipments in real-time, thus reducing dispatchers' workloads.

10. Maintenance Tracking Software (MTS)

This software optimizes many areas of vehicle maintenance. For example, MTS can track and reorder parts in a repair department or do real-time vehicle diagnostic via satellite communications. As real-time information becomes available about the performance of trucks, MTS is used to continuously improve the performance of vehicles and schedule preventive and emergency repairs as needed in the most cost-effective manner.

11. Internet

The Internet provides a variety of communications opportunities. Its current most common application allows for low-cost computer-to-computer messaging and data sharing. EDI is viable via the Internet, replacing the higher-cost proprietary telecommunications networks.

ESTIMATION OF COST EFFECTS FOR POTENTIAL TRANS-CONTINENTAL RAILROAD MERGERS

C. Gregory Bereskin

ABSTRACT

Following the movement toward deregulation of the transportation industry in the late 1970s and early 1980s, the industry experienced a series of mergers. One of the primary claims with regard to merger proposals was that the industry was characterized by significant economies of scale, scope, and density that could be extracted by the larger firms.

This paper examines the effects on railroad costs of four potential transcontinental railroad mergers. Using a translog functional form, a cost function is estimated for a sample of railroads. The cost model is then simulated using the traffic data from each of the actual and (by summation) merged firms to estimate what the firms' costs might be were such combinations to obtain. The hypothetical costs of the merged firms are examined in order to evaluate the efficiency effects of the mergers.

INTRODUCTION

Prior to 1980, the merging of two railroads was a drawn-out activity. With passage of the Staggers Rail Act in 1980, the rules changed allowing for much easier and faster consolidation of railroads. In 1978, there were thirty-seven

Transportation After Deregulation, Volume 6, pages 97–120.

ISBN: 0-7623-0780-3

Class I railroads in the United States. By 1999, there are only seven Class Is. The industry is, however, somewhat more concentrated than this number suggests being dominated by four large railroads, two western railroads (the Burlington-Northern-Santa-Fe and the Union Pacific systems) and two eastern railroads (the Norfolk-Southern and the CSX systems) with three smaller roads in between. One of the arguments for the consolidation was that the technology of the railroad industry could be characterized by economies of scale, scope, and density. Unfortunately, there has been, however, little research to indicate whether cost savings from larger systems would actually accrue with mergers.

Most of the economic models such as those of Caves, Christensen, and Swanson; Spady and Friedlaender; and Bereskin have concentrated on the shape of the cost function and its implications for productivity growth and economies of scale, scope and density. Oum and Waters have discussed the status of transportation cost research advances over the last two decades and have described various refinements in the modeling methodology that has allowed researchers to further test for economies of scale n achieving productivity gains both over time and through mergers and that rail costs are decidedly non-linear in nature.

Over the same period, the rail industry and the government (specifically the Interstate Commerce Commission (ICC) and the current Surface Transportation Board (STB)) have been concerned with developing models that can be used for costing specific traffic, having less concern for the economic characteristics of the model. Examples of the latter method include Rail Form A and the more current Uniform Rail Costing System (URCS). These models use linear "percent variable" equations to allocate expenses to specific operating activities. Three primary problems exist with these regulatory models. First, the allocative equations apply only one measure of intermediate activity; second, the models are linear in nature; and third, neither of these models has been updated since the late 1980s and the estimated parameters may be significantly out of date. McCullough has attacked the problem from a different direction by using instruments created from an aggregation of car-mile types to relate costs to car-miles in order to determine costs characteristics for railroad traffic.

This study involves the development of a model of railroad costs that may be applied toward the analysis of railroads in merger situations. The model is estimated using a set of data on Class I railroad expenditures over the period 1983 to 1999. The model is then used to project costs for each of the four major railroads individually, based on their 1999 traffic levels, and for four possible combined transcontinental systems made up of the current two large eastern and two large western railroads. Cost estimates for the transcontinental systems are then compared with the estimates for the un-merged firms to evaluate whether efficiencies are expected to obtain.

METHODOLOGY

The Cost Function

For purposes of the current analysis, the cost function will be modeled using the translog specification. This is a common procedure in developing economic models of rail costs as the translog is one of a group of functions classified as "flexible functional forms" which, under specific assumptions concerning the coefficients, may be seen to approximate unknown underlying functions. In its translog form, the basic cost function may be written:

$$\ln C = a_{00} + \sum_{i=1}^{N} a_i \ln Q_i + \sum_{h=1}^{H} a_{x_h} \ln x_h + \sum_{j=1}^{M} a_j \ln P_j^h + \sum_{i=1}^{N}\sum_{k=1}^{N} b_{ik} \ln Q_i \ln Q_k$$
$$+ \sum_{i=1}^{N}\sum_{h=1}^{H} b_{ix_h} \ln Q_i \ln x_h + \sum_{j=1}^{M}\sum_{h=1}^{H} b_{jx_h} \ln x_h \ln P_j^h + \sum_{i=1}^{N}\sum_{j=1}^{M} b_{ij} \ln Q_i \ln P_j^h$$
$$+ \sum_{h=1}^{H}\sum_{g=1}^{H} b_{hh} \ln x_h \ln x_g + \sum_{j=1}^{M}\sum_{l=1}^{M} b_{jm} \ln P_j^h \ln P_m^h + T \qquad (1)$$

where $Q = (Q_1, Q_2, \ldots, Q_N)$ is a vector of intermediate measures of output which when combined define the characteristics of the final output,[1] $P^h = (P_1, P_2, \ldots, P_M)$ is a vector of factor input prices, excluding the price of the fixed factors x_h, such that p_j is the price of factor input x_j, and T is a vector of technological factors.

Technological Variations in the Model

Technological variation (other than that implied by the structure of the model itself) both over time and across firms is of importance in the development and estimation of the model. It is assumed that these variations may be described as the combination of two terms one relating to time and a second related to inter-firm differences. The time-shift factor is assumed to account for technological changes in the production process that are occurring over time and which are thus directly reflective of the rate of change in productivity.

The inter-firm variations are accounted for through the use of shift parameters on a firm by firm basis. For notational simplicity, these terms have been included in a vector "T" and are reflective of the differences in operating philosophy, territory, terrain, local conditions, and the mix of traffic which would cause the commonly defined activity variables to be slightly different across firms, rather than being directly reflective, alone, of the economies that may occur from the combination of firms. The general cost function will then be written:

$$C = (Q, P^h, x_h; T) = z(T) * C(Q, P^h, x_h) \quad (2)$$

A further assumption is that the time and industry portions of this vector are multiplicative in nature so that the technology function may be developed as:

$$z(T) = e^{time} * z_f(T) \quad (3)$$

where the subscripts f refers to the individual firm variable.

By substituting (3) into (2) and taking the natural log of (2) the cost function becomes:

$$\ln C = \ln C(Q, P^h, x_h) + \ln z_f(T) + time \quad (4)$$

where shift parameters are applied in an additive manner to the translog cost model.

Use of the translog function requires that certain restrictions are met in order to insure that the cost function is well behaved as required by economic theory. A primary requirement is that the cost function should be linearly homogeneous in input prices. As such, the regression model requires restrictions on the price related coefficients within the cost equation. These restrictions may be written:

$$\sum_{j=1}^{n} a_j = 1 \quad (5a)$$

$$\sum_{j=1}^{M} b_{jl} = 0 \quad \forall \; l = x_h; i = 1, \ldots, N; j = 1, \ldots, M \quad (5b)$$

where the a_j terms correspond to the coefficients on the linear price terms of the translog equation and the b_{jl} values are the coefficients for the quadratic price related variables in the translog specification. Symmetry conditions indicate that $b_{jl} = b_{lj}$.

The variables included in the model are described in Table 1. Four input prices are included: the prices of labor as measured by wages and supplements, the price of materials and supplies by the index for materials and supply excluding fuel, the price of fuel as indicated by the fuel price index, and the price of other items indicated by the AAR's index for other expenses. Output is measured by a combination of intermediate operating measures: gross-ton-miles, car-miles, train-miles, locomotive-horsepower-miles, and total-switching-hours. Through the use of five measures of output simultaneously, it is expected that the cost differences due to varying traffic patterns may be sufficiently accounted for.[2] As is common in much of the transportation literature plant size is accounted for by the measure of miles-of-road operated. Road and track mileage are often acknowledged as one of the, though not a perfect, measures

Table 1. Definition of Variables.

C = TOT_EXP	Total railroad operating expenses
GTMC	Gross-ton-miles of cars, contents, and cabooses for firm f at time t (in millions)
CM:	Car-miles for firm f at time t.
TM:	Train-miles for firm f at time t.
THP	Thousands of horsepower miles (locomotive unit miles * average horsepower)
THS	Total switching hours (road-switching + yard switching)
MR:	The miles of rail operated by firm "f" at time "t" – a proxy variable for the fixed factors of production.
TR:	The miles of track operated by firm "f" at time "t" – a proxy variable for the fixed factors of production.
PF:	Price index for fuel (applicable only to the transportation sector)
PWS:	Price index for wages and supplement.
PMS:	Price index for materials and supplies.
PO:	Price index for other operating expenses.
d(firm #):	Firm proxy variable to compensate for inter-firm variation of non-merger firms.***
D_rr_#	Separate dummy variables representing firms where mergers have occurred. Each firm is indicated by a pre-merger number and a post merger number. Mergers are assumed to have occurred when the reporting entities are changed.
D_rr_sc#	Dummy variable to account for special charges to expenses as taken by a specific railroad in a specific year. Some railroads have booked more than one special charge.
Time	Time variable for underlying productivity trend experienced over the whole data period.

** The natural log of any of the specific mnemonics above is indicated by prefixing with the letter L: For example: LMOW = log (MOW). This convention will be followed throughout the paper. Squared terms are indicated by a 2 at the name end while cross terms are indicated by a combination of the two names with the second 'L' deleted. For example, LGTMC * LCM = LGTMCM and LCM * LCM = LCM2.

*** The Illinois Central railroad has been deleted from the sample for the years 1997, a year in which the railroad reported zero switching hours.

**** For 1999, Conrail reported output measures separately for five months. These have been divided equally between Norfolk-Southern and CSX to get annual values.

of capital for the railroads. Development and use of an alternative series is beyond the scope of the current study and, historically in railroad costing, it has been commonly believed that measures such as these are sufficient for regulatory and other purposes.

DATA AND ESTIMATION – PRIVATE COSTS

During the long period of railroad regulation, the interstate Commerce Commission (ICC) required the railroads to supply information on their costs and expenditures. Following deregulation, the Association of American Railroads (AAR) has continued to maintain many of the data series on railroad operations. This effort provided an unusually valuable data source. The data as collected by the AAR are available through their two publications "Analysis of Class I Railroads" and the "Railroad Cost Recovery Indexes" which supplies indices of input prices. Using these two sources, a fairly complete picture of rail operations may be developed.

The data are limited to the period 1983 through 1999 due to the accounting change from Retirement, Replacement, Betterment accounting to Depreciation accounting which began with the 1983 reporting year. An additional data problem involves the shrinking number of railroads as mergers or bankruptcies occurred and as some firms were dropped due to insufficient revenues to remain classified as Class I. Where mergers occurred, dummy variables for the firms prior to and following the merger were included in the model to act as proxies for changing railroad structure. As each merger was concluded, a new dummy variable was created using the railroad name and a higher number. For example, when the Union Pacific added the Missouri Pacific and Western Pacific the variable D_UP_1 ended and D_UP_2 began . Likewise, a number of special accounting charges were taken over the twenty-one year period. In each year where a firm took a special charge against expenses this was modeled with a 0,1 dummy variable. The rationale for modeling the charges this way was to allow the remaining variables to operate more freely within the model to explain costs rather than modifying the data set to reflect charges that may not be directly related to the level of the firm's operations in any given year.

The data set as constituted consisted of seventeen years of observations with 29 firms before consolidation. After consolidation and removal of several firms from the list of Class I railroads due to reduction in comparative revenues, the final year (1999) consisted of data for only seven firms. Constructing the data in this manner gave 257 observations on a varying number of firms per year for the seventeen years, a large enough sample to provide sufficient degrees of freedom for most estimation techniques associated with pooled data.

The model was estimated for the translog functional form (Eq. 1) of the cost model. In addition to the cost function, Shephard's Lemma was applied to develop factor share equations for fuel, labor (wages and supplements), and other operating expenses.[3] Simultaneous estimation of the cost model and the factor share equation was performed using a full-information-maximum-likelihood algorithm. The causal variables consisted of the parameters for gross-ton miles; car-miles; train-miles; thousands-of-horsepower-miles; total-switching-hours; miles-of-road operated; miles-of-track operated; input price indices for fuel, wages and supplements, materials and supplies, and other expenses; and the dummy variables representing individual firms, mergers, and special charges. The firm dummies and special charge dummies were not included as quadratic terms in the translog functional relationship but appear as 0,1 shift parameters. The restrictions on the regression equations were required in order to insure linear homogeneity of the input prices within the cost function.[4] Results of these regressions are included in Table 2. The regression results are reasonable for a translog specification. One concern when using the translog form is over the number of variables whose t-statistics indicate a weak level of significance. This is not an uncommon situation when a complete translog function is estimated due to the large number of factors included in the functional form and the general close relationship of the variables which is expected to cause some degree of multicollinearity. As long as each individual variable (gtmc, tm, cm, etc.) is important and included, the choices for getting desirable t-statistics are limited. One possibility is to individually parse the regression terms until only statistically significant terms remain. This method may cause the translog to loose its validity as an approximation to an unknown underlying function. Since all of the variables are believed to be important cost related elements in the movement of trains and the factors as a group were significant to the regression, each of the variables was left in the equation.

A further consideration included in the evaluation of the regression involved the values and signs and sizes of the partial elasticity estimates shown in Table 3a and 3b that resulted from the regression equation. As would be expected the values of the partial elasticities were each generally between zero and one, a pattern that is normal and desirable. It must be remembered that none of the variables will work completely independently as, for example, an increase in gross-ton-miles will frequently be accompanied by increased car-miles, train-miles, and locomotive-horsepower-miles.

The partial elasticity estimates relative to the price variables sum to unity indicating that the linear homogenity conditions are met. Summing the partial elasticity values relative to the five activity measures yields a value less than one indicating economies to increasing output around the point measured. This relationship is commonly defined in the transportation industry as economies of density. As output increases relative to a constant network size, average cost per unit of output is seen to decrease. As done here, the intermediate activity measures may all be increased by a multiplicative factor while holding miles-

Table 2. Regression Results.

Variable	Coefficient	Std. Error	T-stat	Significance
^CONST	14.571400	7.470090	1.950640	0.052000
LGTM	−0.492207	1.612850	−0.305179	0.760000
LCM	3.194070	3.321600	0.961605	0.337000
LTM	−3.360680	3.107730	−1.081390	0.281000
LTHP	0.761001	1.462910	0.520198	0.603000
LTHS	−0.165301	0.214452	−0.770808	0.442000
LMR	−2.142120	1.135450	−1.886590	0.060000
LTR	−0.000024	0.000008	−2.921100	0.004000
LPF	−0.088282	0.042717	−2.066660	0.040000
LPWS	1.376260	0.129542	10.624000	0.000000
LPO	−0.439050	0.222690	−1.971570	0.050000
LGTM2	0.008641	0.067452	0.128106	0.898000
LGTMCM	−0.387468	0.463750	−0.835512	0.404000
LGTMTM	0.655633	0.536262	1.222600	0.223000
LGTMTHP	−0.301578	0.298757	−1.009440	0.314000
LGTMTHS	0.038962	0.054263	0.718012	0.473000
LGTMMR	0.993250	0.499963	1.986650	0.048000
LGTMTR	−0.951655	0.513072	−1.854820	0.065000
LGTMPF	0.001412	0.006451	0.218825	0.827000
LGTMPWS	−0.031287	0.024379	−1.283390	0.201000
LGTMPO	0.040778	0.028800	1.415900	0.158000
LCM2	0.410181	0.457670	0.896237	0.371000
LCMTM	−0.989138	0.886597	−1.115660	0.266000
LCMTHP	0.528171	0.395938	1.333970	0.183000
LCMTHS	−0.039907	0.054140	−0.737107	0.462000
LCMMR	0.020974	0.554002	0.037858	0.970000
LCMTR	−0.027451	0.613871	−0.044718	0.964000
LCMPF	−0.010561	0.009280	−1.138030	0.256000
LCMPWS	0.089524	0.030583	2.927240	0.004000
LCMPO	−0.110281	0.036504	−3.021100	0.003000
LTM2	0.263121	0.328706	0.800476	0.424000
LTMTHP	−0.247659	0.375422	−0.659683	0.510000
LTMTHS	0.035030	0.043634	0.802826	0.423000
LTMMR	−0.902535	0.569687	−1.584270	0.114000
LTMTR	0.931284	0.604065	1.541700	0.124000
LTMPF	0.012364	0.007758	1.593590	0.112000
LTMPWS	−0.106285	0.029473	−3.606210	0.000000
LTMPO	0.084733	0.034947	2.424630	0.016000
LTHP2	0.102141	0.179489	0.569068	0.570000
LTHPTHS	−0.047294	0.029702	−1.592270	0.113000
LTHPMR	0.149564	0.474688	0.315078	0.753000
LTHPTR	−0.315903	0.519802	−0.607738	0.544000
LTHPPF	0.018669	0.004344	4.297970	0.000000
LTHPPWS	−0.033203	0.015202	−2.184210	0.030000

Table 2. Continued.

Variable	Coefficient	Std. Error	T-stat	Significance
LTHPPO	0.023522	0.017091	1.376320	0.170000
LTHS2	−0.000132	0.000839	−0.156919	0.875000
LTHSMR	−0.026476	0.037384	−0.708230	0.479000
LTHSTR	0.060409	0.041033	1.472200	0.142000
LTHSPF	−0.002497	0.000894	−2.791700	0.006000
LTHSPWS	−0.004691	0.002922	−1.605280	0.110000
LTHSPO	0.009388	0.003166	2.965440	0.003000
LMR2	0.258121	0.212811	1.212910	0.226000
LMRTR	−0.875910	0.404919	−2.163170	0.031000
LMRPF	0.035528	0.007317	4.855420	0.000000
LMRPWS	−0.025224	0.017252	−1.462120	0.145000
LMRPO	−0.037445	0.012429	−3.012670	0.003000
LTR2	0.838531	0.267444	3.135350	0.002000
LTRPF	−0.057609	0.007234	−7.963840	0.000000
LTRPWS	0.109844	0.014665	7.490450	0.000000
LTRPO	−0.012018	0.016258	−0.739175	0.460000
LPF2	0.031350	0.002880	10.883700	0.000000
LPFPWS	−0.027028	0.015206	−1.777470	0.077000
LPFPO	−0.025543	0.015851	−1.611490	0.108000
LPWS2	0.069186	0.016250	4.257580	0.000000
LPWSPO	−0.011248	0.013272	−0.847522	0.397000
LPO2	−0.034568	0.020600	−1.678080	0.095000
D03	−0.178303	0.289266	−0.616398	0.538000
D04	−0.171345	0.139123	−1.231610	0.219000
D06	0.193520	0.089012	2.174100	0.031000
D07	−0.033147	0.042481	−0.780284	0.436000
D08	−0.217639	0.055078	−3.951480	0.000000
D12	0.008930	0.067665	0.131968	0.895000
D13	−0.376065	0.130798	−2.875160	0.004000
D14	−0.243308	0.063409	−3.837100	0.000000
D15	−0.361755	0.164869	−2.194190	0.029000
D16	−0.200992	0.190439	−1.055420	0.292000
D17	−0.438276	0.520351	−0.842270	0.400000
D18	−0.687007	0.150254	−4.572300	0.000000
D21	−0.086860	0.042695	−2.034440	0.043000
D22	−0.232163	0.041243	−5.629160	0.000000
D25	−0.255875	0.071107	−3.598460	0.000000
D26	−0.015556	0.062213	−0.250048	0.803000
D27	0.065488	0.068198	0.960277	0.338000
D28	0.036016	0.274343	0.131279	0.896000
D30	−0.289916	0.069707	−4.159070	0.000000
D34	−0.045442	0.055940	−0.812330	0.417000
D37	−0.304362	0.064460	−4.721690	0.000000
D_BN_3	−0.180448	0.058775	−3.07017460	0.002000

Table 2. Continued.

Variable	Coefficient	Std. Error	T-stat	Significance
D_BN_4	−0.037436	0.057182	−0.654678	0.513000
D_BO_2	0.115487	0.062079	1.860330	0.064000
D_GTW_2	0.264686	0.042677	6.202130	0.000000
D_SCL_2	−0.014163	0.061534	−0.230168	0.818000
D_SOO_1	−0.275232	0.083720	−3.287550	0.001000
D_SOO_2	−0.212283	0.047439	−4.474850	0.000000
D_SP_1	0.088901	0.051215	1.735840	0.084000
D_SP_2	0.019781	0.050639	0.390619	0.696000
D_SP_3	−0.051278	0.066474	−0.771397	0.441000
D_UP_1	0.021738	0.049432	0.439763	0.660000
D_UP_2	−0.143803	0.062855	−2.287860	0.023000
D_UP_3	−0.168696	0.051473	−3.277330	0.001000
D_UP_4	−0.184957	0.062775	−2.946370	0.004000
D_UP_5	0.060206	0.056543	1.064770	0.288000
D_CSX	0.032108	0.051375	0.624967	0.533000
D_NS	0.018601	0.046521	0.399837	0.690000
D01_SC1	−0.003962	0.057759	−0.068592	0.945000
D01_SC2	0.097305	0.051179	1.901250	0.058000
D01_SC3	−0.007664	0.054200	−0.141403	0.888000
D05_SC1	−0.020036	0.046891	−0.427286	0.670000
D05_SC2	0.046448	0.046048	1.008690	0.314000
D05_SC3	0.042301	0.053697	0.787766	0.432000
D05_SC4	0.007595	0.062392	0.121728	0.903000
D07_SC1	0.028496	0.049620	0.574291	0.566000
D07_SC2	−0.052983	0.049646	−1.067220	0.287000
D_90	−0.004128	0.019353	−0.213298	0.831000
D07_SC3	−0.556618	0.902485	−0.616762	0.538000
D07_SC4	−0.165265	0.050248	−3.288950	0.001000
D07_SC5	−0.145758	0.050120	−2.908210	0.004000
D12_SC1	−0.024895	0.051769	−0.480875	0.631000
D12_SC2	0.004652	0.048991	0.094949	0.924000
D12_SC3	0.144768	0.072139	2.006790	0.046000
D12_SC4	0.106763	0.050271	2.123740	0.035000
D12_SC5	0.080151	0.051358	1.560650	0.120000
D12_SC6	0.291636	0.057740	5.050820	0.000000
D14_SC1	−0.014503	0.060601	−0.239323	0.811000
D20_SC1	0.121537	0.052710	2.305770	0.022000
D20_SC2	−0.032258	0.050956	−0.633062	0.527000
D20_SC3	0.164170	0.051449	3.190920	0.002000
D20_SC4	0.157221	0.059046	2.662680	0.008000
D20_SC5	−0.152616	0.059332	−2.572220	0.011000
D21_SC1	0.448835	0.256024	1.753100	0.081000
D21_SC2	−0.007825	0.045757	−0.171019	0.864000
D22_SC1	0.048716	0.049463	0.984887	0.326000

Table 2. Continued.

Variable	Coefficient	Std. Error	T-stat	Significance
D22_SC2	0.176336	0.048379	3.644910	0.000000
D30_SC1	0.123775	0.058426	2.118510	0.035000
D32_SC1	−0.022261	0.052337	−0.425334	0.671000
D32_SC2	−0.018130	0.048422	−0.374417	0.708000
D32_SC3	0.004762	0.048558	0.098071	0.922000
D32_SC4	0.121902	0.056242	2.167430	0.031000
D32_SC5	0.200202	0.067775	2.953900	0.003000
D32_SC6	0.070538	0.057093	1.235490	0.218000
D33_SC1	0.077783	0.057724	1.347500	0.179000
D33_SC2	0.040753	0.048112	0.847040	0.398000
D33_SC3	−0.339091	0.073079	−4.640040	0.000000
D35_SC1	0.018260	0.045408	0.402144	0.688000
D42_SC1	−0.017845	0.046446	−0.384207	0.701000
D42_SC2	−0.051840	0.043270	−1.198070	0.232000
D43_SC1	0.024049	0.046320	0.519190	0.604000
D43_SC2	−0.010854	0.042012	−0.258353	0.796000
D43_SC3	−0.004839	0.043138	−0.112176	0.911000
D12_SC7	0.163644	0.053885	3.036880	0.003000
D32_SC7	−0.147001	0.065249	−2.252940	0.025000
D42_SC3	0.010444	0.044462	0.234898	0.814000
D42_SC4	0.037568	0.052134	0.720601	0.472000
D43_SC4	0.107113	0.061116	1.752610	0.081000
TIME	−0.027183	0.002713	−10.018700	0.000000

Log of Likelihood Function = 3683.17.

Cost Function
Eq. TOTAL_EXP; Dependent variable is LTOT_EXP; R-Squared = 0.993805; No. obs = 257; Durbin-Watson (29 gaps) = 1.233784; Sum of squared residuals = 2.60351; Std. error of regression = 0.100650; Sum of residuals = −0.687321E-01; Mean of dependent variable = 13.6836.

Factor Share Equations
Eq. FS_F_TOT (Factor Share Fuel); Dependent variable is FSTOT_F; R-Squared = 0.691987; No. obs = 257; Durbin-Watson (29 gaps) = 0.766550; Sum of squared residuals = 0.488441E-01; Std. error of regression = 0.137860E-01; Sum of residuals = 0.216050E-01; Mean of dependent variable = 0.803042E-01.

Eq. FS_WS_TOT (Factor Share Wages and Supplements); Dependent variable is FSTOT_WS; R-Squared = 0.359407; No. obs = 257; Durbin-Watson (29 gaps) = 1.136802; Sum of squared residuals = 0.960299; Std. error of regression = 0.611275E-01; Sum of residuals = −0.732567E-02; Mean of dependent variable = 0.458311.

Eq. FS_O_TOT (Factor Share Other expenses); Dependent variable is FSTOT_O; R-Squared = 0.247417; No. obs = 257; Durbin-Watson (29 gaps) = 1.144962; Sum of squared residuals = 1.28241; Std. error of regression = 0.706393E-01; Sum of residuals = −0.221740E-01; Mean of dependent variable = 0.389175.

Table 3. Definition of Railroad Operating Parameters, 1999.

RRNAME	BN	UP	CSX	NS	BN_CSX	BN_NS	UP_CSX	UP_NS
GTMC	8.7195E+08	9.0639E+08	4.4957E+08	3.5918E+08	1.3215E+09	1.2311E+09	1.3560E+09	1.2656E+09
CM	8.9899E+06	1.2846E+07	5.5808E+06	4.5601E+06	1.4571E+07	1.3550E+07	1.8426E+07	1.7406E+07
TM	1.4610E+08	1.5597E+08	9.1496E+07	6.9563E+07	2.3759E+08	2.1566E+08	2.4746E+08	2.2553E+08
THP	1.4777E+09	1.7719E+09	6.5396E+08	5.7677E+08	2.1316E+09	2.0544E+09	2.4259E+09	2.3487E+09
THS	2.5852E+06	4.4560E+06	3.0575E+06	3.5521E+06	5.6427E+06	6.1373E+06	7.5135E+06	8.0081E+06
MR	3.3264E+04	3.3341E+04	2.3357E+04	2.1788E+04	5.6621E+04	5.5052E+04	5.6698E+04	5.5129E+04
TR	5.0759E+04	5.5001E+04	4.0683E+04	3.8708E+04	9.1442E+04	8.9467E+04	9.5684E+04	9.3709E+04
P_F	1.6470E+02	1.6470E+02	1.4322E+02	1.4322E+02	1.5396E+02	1.5396E+02	1.5396E+02	1.5396E+02
P_WS	3.0360E+02	3.0360E+02	3.0900E+02	3.0900E+02	3.0630E+02	3.0630E+02	3.0630E+02	3.0630E+02
P_O	1.9330E+02	1.9330E+02	1.9330E+02	1.9330E+02	1.9330E+02	1.9330E+02	1.9330E+02	1.9330E+02
P_MS	2.3080E+02	2.3080E+02	1.7960E+02	1.7960E+02	2.0520E+02	2.0520E+02	2.0520E+02	2.0520E+02

Table 3a. Partial Elasticity of Cost Estimates Relative to Intermediate Activity Measures.

RR_Name	GTMC	CM	TM	THP	THS
BN	0.207808	0.288324	0.124703	0.083385	0.030645
UP	0.005404	0.573479	-0.121758	0.230353	0.016257
CSX	0.188021	0.173378	0.230611	-0.011138	0.042790
NS	0.104735	0.293315	0.191790	-0.009684	0.037240
BN_CSX	0.235678	0.197573	0.177407	0.023661	0.048934
BN_NS	0.206357	0.238423	0.168930	0.021843	0.046826
UP_CSX	0.102192	0.395601	0.002484	0.128573	0.038505
UP_NS	0.066444	0.447741	-0.019071	0.135034	0.035836

Table 3b. Partial Elasticity of Cost Estimates Relative to Size and Input Prices.

RR_Name	MR	TR	P_F	P_WS	P_O	P_MS
BN	0.313046	0.801642	0.083120	0.373707	0.360549	0.182624
UP	0.243658	0.923945	0.077703	0.397672	0.336641	0.187984
CSX	-0.059845	1.235650	0.059285	0.443704	0.321563	0.175448
NS	-0.054750	1.225770	0.055390	0.461527	0.313119	0.169964
BN_CSX	0.084628	1.307780	0.071223	0.402471	0.343578	0.182728
BN_NS	0.097024	1.291720	0.070053	0.407621	0.341727	0.180598
UP_CSX	0.051121	1.366050	0.068418	0.417668	0.327319	0.186595
UP_NS	0.062424	1.350510	0.067217	0.423780	0.324066	0.184937

of-road (MR) and miles-of-track (TR) constant. As the partial elasticities sum to less than unity, this indicates that as all activity measures increase by the same percentage, cost increases by a lesser percentage so that average cost declines.

SIMULATION AND RESULTS

Following estimation of the model, the equation may be used for simulation of the cost structure of each of the individual firms in the sample and, as developed here, combinations of various railroads. The operating parameters, miles of road and track and price indices for 1999 are given in Table 3. For the merged railroads (BN_CSX, BN_NS, UP_CSX, AND UP_CSX) the values of the individual partners have been summed. This initially disallows for any change in the type of traffic carried following the potential mergers but does allow for a reasonable evaluation of the economies/diseconomies that may result from the combinations.

To further examine potential efficiencies, the merged firms are allowed variations resulting from the technological variables included in the regression. Since each firm is characterized by a 0,1 dummy variable in the regression model (indicating a shift in the cost function), the value used in the simulation is initially indeterminate for the merged firms. Two possible solutions are examined here. First, the shift parameter for the merged firm is taken as an average of the values of the two merger partners. Second, using the optimistic assumption that the merged firm will eventually look like the lower cost member of the merger, the smaller of the two shift values is used to estimate costs under an "efficient firm" assumption. Results of these two simulations showing estimates of total cost, cost per gross ton miles, costs per car mile and cost per train mile are shown in Table 4 and Graphs A through D. As would be expected the "efficient" firm model shows slightly lower costs under all scenarios.

In order to examine what might happen to transportation costs as traffic levels vary (beyond the level of the combinations due to the potential mergers), an additional simulation of the "efficient" firm model was accomplished. In this simulation, the traffic level for each firm was allowed to vary from 0.8 times its estimated level for 1999 to 2.0 times that level by increments of 0.1. The results of this simulation, both for the actual firms and for the potentially merged firms are graphed in Graph E. As might be expected, the simulations show the potential for significant economies to output and to firm size. One caveat to this analysis is that the type of traffic and therefore the relationship between the five intermediate measures of activity that go into making up the output measure is assumed to be constant over the simulation. While the basic conclusion of economies is expected to continue to hold, it is important to remember that in reality, as firms merge the mix of traffic will vary from historic patterns. For example, one argument for mergers is that the increased route mileage and potential for longer hauls will lead to greater operating efficiencies. Thus, the ratios of gross-ton-miles, train-miles, car-miles, locomotive-horsepower-miles and switching hours to miles-of-road and miles-of-track will change were any of the mergers to actually occur. As a result, actual merger results would be expected to vary from the simulations. These simulations further strengthen the view that the industry is experiencing economies of scale.

Table 4. Cost Estimates for the Average and "Efficient" Merged Railroads.

	Efficient Merged				Average Merged			
RR_NAME	TOT_COST	COST/GTMC	COST/CM	COST/TM	TOT_COST	COST/GTMC	COST/CM	COST/TM
BN	6.75945E+06	7.75209E-03	7.51890E-01	4.62665E-02	6.75945E+06	7.75209E-03	7.51890E-01	4.62665E-02
UP	8.82335E+06	9.73456E-03	6.86883E-01	5.65723E-02	8.82335E+06	9.73456E-03	6.86883E-01	5.65723E-02
CSX	4.72754E+06	1.05157E-02	8.47110E-01	5.16694E-02	4.72754E+06	1.05157E-02	8.47110E-01	5.16694E-02
NS	4.04790E+06	1.12698E-02	8.87681E-01	5.81902E-02	4.04790E+06	1.12698E-02	8.87681E-01	5.81902E-02
BN_CSX	7.28347E+06	5.51142E-03	4.99870E-01	3.06551E-02	7.54118E+06	5.70644E-03	5.17557E-01	.17398E-02
BN_NS	7.07319E+06	5.74527E-03	5.22006E-01	3.27977E-02	7.27203E+06	5.90678E-03	5.36680E-01	3.37197E-02
UP_CSX	8.29391E+06	6.11662E-03	4.50113E-01	3.35159E-02	8.41126E+06	6.20316E-03	4.56481E-01	3.39901E-02
UP_NS	8.06271E+06	6.37079E-03	4.63225E-01	3.57502E-02	8.23462E+06	6.50662E-03	4.73102E-01	3.65124E-02

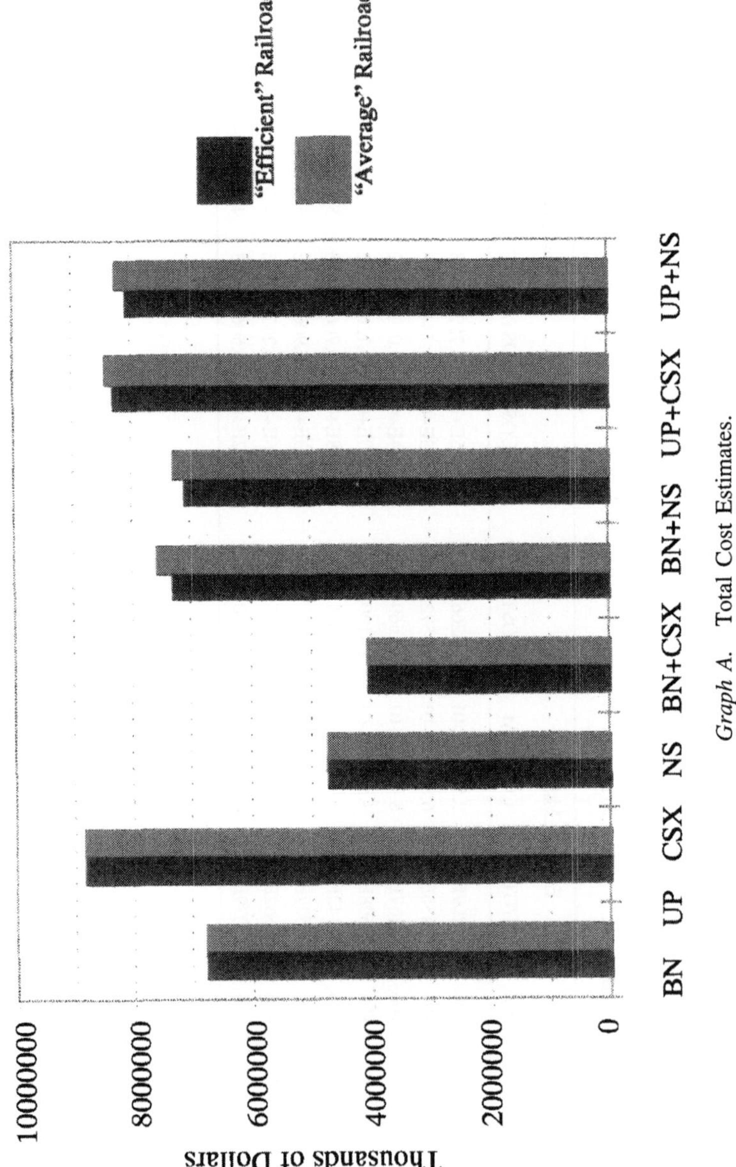

Graph A. Total Cost Estimates.

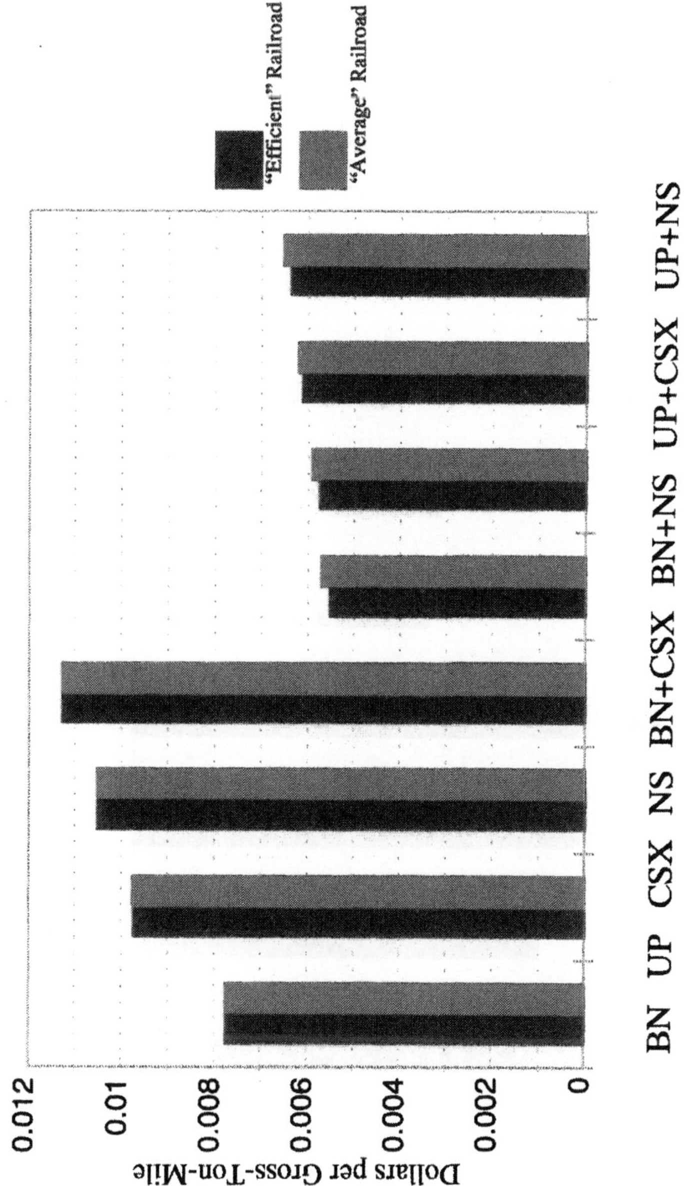

Graph B. Cost Estimates: Per Gros-Ton-Mile.

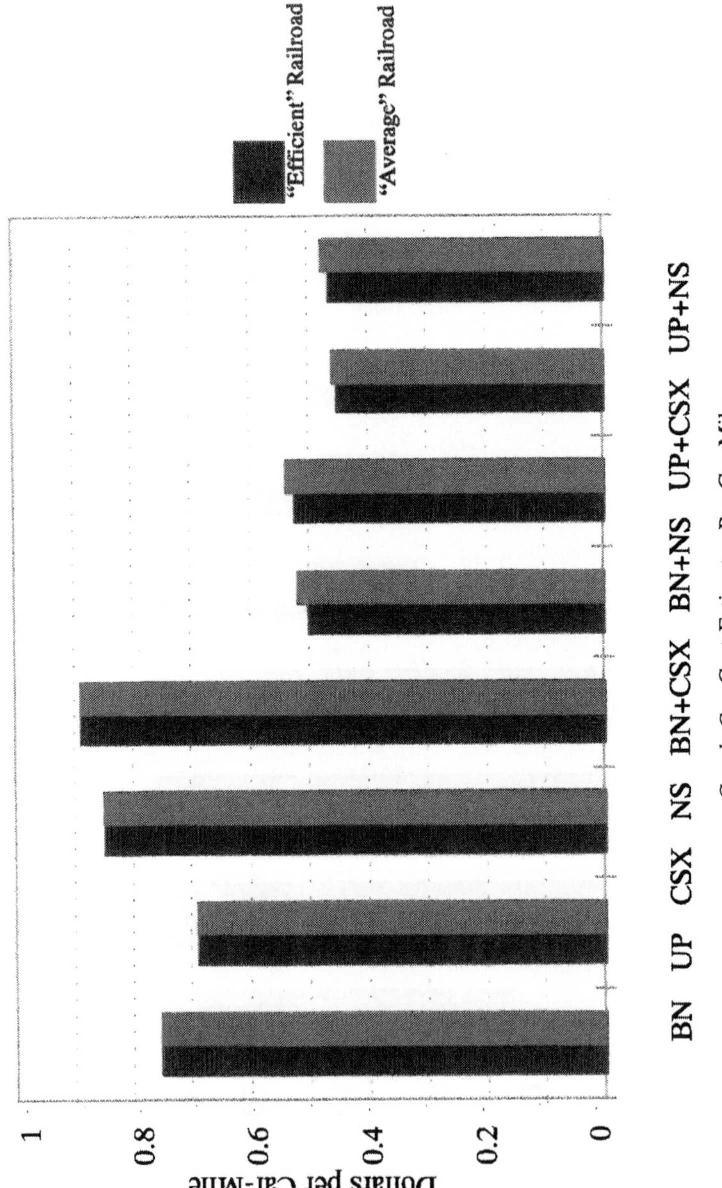

Graph C. Cost Estimates Per Car-Mile.

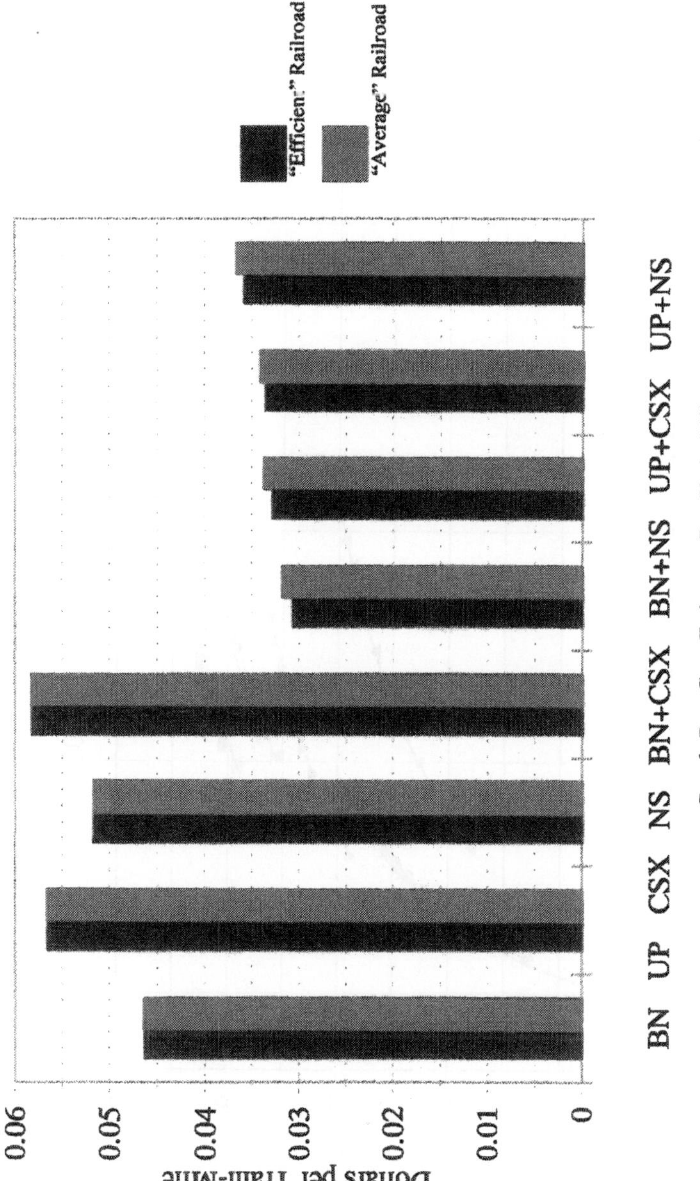

Graph D. Cost Estimates Per Train-Mile.

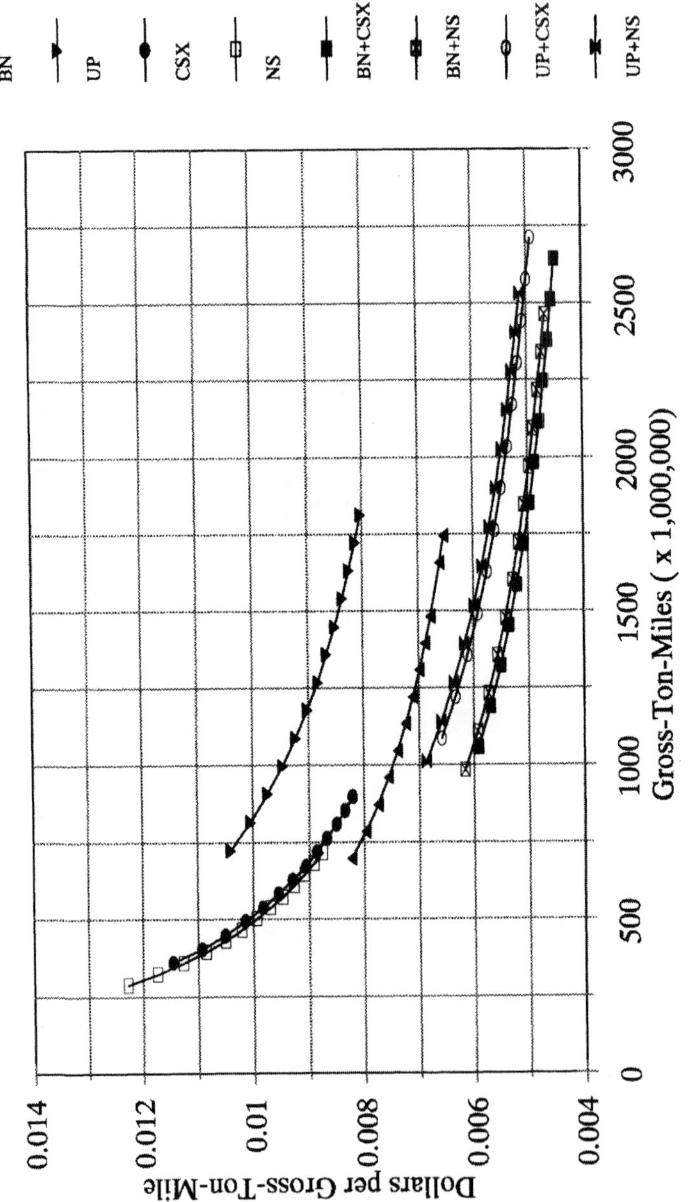

Graph E. Simulated Costs 0.8 to 2.0 × Traffic.

CONCLUSIONS

The research presented here has several important implications in terms of costing of railroad traffic and railroad mergers. First, the model demonstrates that, with only minor simplifying assumptions, a general model of total railroad costs may be estimated and used to evaluate costing efficiencies from mergers. Through simulation analysis, it is possible to look at different combinations and evaluate the effect of economies of scale. The costs may be used for analysis of competitive market conditions, analysis of individual train costs or analysis of changes in road structure on costs.

Second, the model demonstrates that cost economies do appear to accrue to larger railroads. Under each of the differing merger scenarios tested, the merged railroad that had more track mileage and greater total traffic also had lower estimated costs per unit of traffic. These are all hypothetical coasts on hypothetical merged railroads (although the analysis is based on actual cost modeling) so the actual costs on actual properties may be expected to vary slightly though not substantially.

Finally, the apparent economies of scale indicate that transcontinental mergers are expected to yield lower operating costs. This does not mean that this research is necessarily in favor of railroad mergers. Company cost considerations are only one of the considerations when evaluating the public benefits and costs of mergers. The question remains as to how much of the projected cost savings would be passed on to consumers in the form of reduced transportation rates. As the number of firms in the industry decreases, choice to consumers may also decrease leading to additional market power for the firm. The translation of higher degrees of market power into higher markups may lead to higher transportation rates. It is also possible, though, that higher markups on lower costs may still yield lower final transportation rates. Net public costs and benefits need to be examined further and with expanded models prior to final evaluation of the desirability of railroad mergers.

NOTES

1. Where joint production occurs such as in the railroad industry it is often impossible to get a single measure of output. Frequently, gross-ton-miles or car-miles are used as proxies. Even when these proxy variables are used, it is appropriate to adjust their values for the variations in traffic level such as was done by McCullouch (1993). As used here, the individual intermediate output measures will be applied directly so that specific final outputs can be described by their characteristics. One potential problem is that the measures may actually reflect different operating characteristics for different

traffic (a thousand car-miles may consist of one car moving a thousand miles or a thousand cars moving one mile). Unfortunately, given the current state of railroad statistics there is little way around this problem which occurs in virtually every rail cost model.

2. There is always some concern over specification bias when estimating any cost function. Through use of these five measures, it is expected that the variability in output has been sufficiently explained especially when compared to models that use single measures of output such as gross-ton-miles alone.

3. A fourth factor share equation for materials and supplies was implicitly used. However inclusion of all four factor share equations in a simultaneous equation model would result in exact multicollinearity of the model. Additionally, the regression coefficients for those terms relating to the price variable (P_MS) for materials and supplies are not directly included in the regression results as these were all defined relative to the other price measures in order to enforce the linear homogeneity conditions as specified by equation 8.

4. The estimation software required that the restrictions be included within the definition of the equations to be estimated. As such, the coefficients on the variables related to the price of materials and supplies are all embedded as linear combinations of other coefficients.

REFERENCES

Bereskin, C. G. (1983). A Bi-Level Model of United States Railroad Costs. Unpublished Doctoral Dissertation, University of Missouri-Columbia.

Bereskin, C. G. (June, 1989). An Econometric Alternative to URCS (Uniform Railroad Costing System). *The Logistics and Transportation Review*, *25*(2), 99–128.

Bereskin, C. G. (Summer, 1996). Econometric Estimation of Post-Deregulation Railway Productivity Growth. Transportation Journal, 35(4), 34–43.

Berndt, E. R., & Christensen, L. R. (1973). The Translog Function and the Substitution of Equipment, Structures, and Labor in the U.S. Manufacturing, 1929–1968. *Journal of Econometrics*, *1*, 81–114.

Berndt, E. R., & Christensen, L. R (1973). The Internal Structure of Functional Relationships: Separability, Substitution, and Aggregation. *Review of Economic Studies*, *40*, 403–410.

Caves, D. W., Christensen, L. R., & Swanson, J. A. (Spring, 1980). Productivity in U.S. Railroads, *1951–1974. Bell Journal of Economics*, 166–181.

Caves, D. W., Christensen, L. R., & Swanson, J. A. (November, 1981b). Economic Performance in Regulated and Unregulated Environments: A Comparison of U.S. and Canadian Railroads. *Quarterly Journal of Economics*, *46*, 559–581.

Caves, D. W., Christensen, L. R., & Swanson, J. A. (December, 1981). Productivity Growth, Scale Economies and Capacity Utilization in U.S. Railroads. 1955–1974. *American Economic Review*, *71*, 994–1002.

Friedlaender, A. F., & Spady, R. H. (June, 1980). Economic Costs and the Uniform Railroad Costing System. *Conference on Railroad Costing Procedures: Interstate Commerce Commission.*

Griliches, Z. (Spring, 1972). Cost Allocation in Railroad Regulation. Bell Journal of Economies, 26–41.

Keeler, T. E. (May, 1974). Railroad Costs, Returns to Scale, and Excess Capacity. Review of *Economics and Statistics*, 201–208.

McCullough, G. J. (1993). *Essays on the Economic Performance of U.S. Freight Railroads Under Deregulation*. Unpublished Doctoral Dissertation, Massachusetts Institute of Technology.

Oum, T. H., & Waters, W. G. II. (December, 1996). A Survey of Recent Developments in Transportation Cost Function Research. *The Logistics and Transportation Review*, *32*(4), 423–463.

Russell, R. R. (1975). Functional Separability and Partial Elasticities of Substitution. *Review of Economic Studies*, *42*, 79–86.

Spady, R. H. (1979). *Econometric Estimation of Cost functions for the Regulated Transportation Industries*. New York: Garland Publishing Inc.

Spady, R. H., & Friedlaender, A. F. (September, 1976). *Economic Estimation of Cost Functions in the Transportation Industries*. Cambridge: MIT Center for Transportation Studies Report Number 76-13.

U.S. Congress, Senate, Committee on Interstate Commerce (1943). *Rail Freight Service Costs in the Various Rate Territories of the United States*. S. Doc. 63, 78th Congress, 1st Session.

APPENDIX

RRID	RAILROAD NAME
01	Atchison Topeka and Santa Fe
02	Baltimore and Ohio
03	Bessemer and Lake Erie
04	Boston and Maine
05	Burlington Northern
06	Chesapeake and Ohio
07	Chicago and Northwestern
08	Chicago, Milwaukee, St Paul, and Pacific
09	Chicago, Rock Island, and Pacific
10	Clinchfield
11	Colorado and Southern
12	Conrail
13	Delaware and Hudson
14	Denver Rio Grande and Western
15	Detroit, Toledo, and Ironton
16	Duluth, Massabi, and Iron Range
17	Elgin, Joliet, and Eastern
18	Florida East Coast
19	Fort Worth and Denver
20	Grand Trunk Western
21	Illinois Central Gulf
22	Kansas City Southern
24	Louisville and Nashville
25	Missouri Kansas Texas
26	Missouri Pacific
27	Norfolk and Western
28	Pittsburgh and Lake Erie
29	St. Louis and San Francisco
30	St. Louis Southwestern
31	Seaboard Coast Line
32	Soo Line
33	Southern Pacific
34	Southern Railway System
35	Union Pacific
36	Western Maryland
37	Western Pacific
42	CSX Corporation
43	Norfolk Southern

RED BUS, GREEN BUS: MARKET ORGANIZATION, DRIVER INCENTIVES, SAFETY, AND SORTING

Frank W. Rusco and W. David Walls

ABSTRACT

We examine minibus competition in Hong Kong between two similar types of minibus firms: those that operate green minibuses and those that operate red minibuses. The two types of firms are distinguished by their industrial organizations and by the restrictions placed on their operations by government regulators and triad societies. Green minibuses are subject to government fare, level of service, and route regulation, and the drivers are paid a fixed monthly salary. Red minibuses are not subject to government fare, level of service, or route regulations, but they are regulated by triad societies, and their drivers are residual claimants who either own or lease their minibus. The institutional and operational characteristics are used to formulate testable implications on accident rates and journey times based on differing driver behavior under these alternative industrial organizations. The empirical results show that red minibuses have a substantially higher accident rate and lower peak-period journey times than do green minibuses, and that green minibuses have slightly lower journey times in the off-peak period. Efficient sorting may imply that passengers with high values of travel time savings and access to both types of buses may choose to ride red minibuses during peak periods and switch to green minibuses in off-peak periods

Transportation After Deregulation, Volume 6, pages 121–142.
2001 by Elsevier Science Ltd.
ISBN: 0-7623-0780-3

1. INTRODUCTION

Transport deregulation has led to an increased interest in the economics of competition in urban transportation markets. Researchers and transport professionals have studied many issues relating to the private provision of public transport,[1] but many important issues remain unresolved. For example, competition between bus operators for passengers in deregulated local bus markets in the United Kingdom has led to an equilibrium where buses tend to cluster together as would occur in a simple Hotelling (1929) model of spatial competition.[2] On the other hand, Foster and Golay (1986) drew on models of spatial competition and concluded that local bus competition would not be disequilibrating under normal circumstances. This paper addresses the impact of differential incentives on driver behavior in a partially deregulated market and the implications of this behavior on the quality and types of bus services and on bus safety.

Our analysis in this paper examines competition between two distinct types of minibus firms and focuses on driver behavior.[3] The two types of firms operate minibuses that are, with the exception of their color, virtually identical in appearance: 16-seat air-conditioned minibuses. However, the organization and operation of the two types of minibus firms differ in numerous ways. Of particular interest is that red minibuses are either owned or leased by the driver, so that the bus driver is the sole claimant to the difference between fares and operating expenses. In contrast, green minibus firms hire drivers on a contract that pays them a fixed wage and grants them no claim to the residual between fares and operating expenses. Also, the government regulates routes, fares, and frequency of service of green minibuses while red minibuses are not constrained to operate under such government regulations. Thus, while two types of buses look nearly identical, the organizational differences create driver incentives that result in measurably heterogeneous services and divergent driver behavior.

In the following section we provide institutional and operational details of minibuses in Hong Kong. We also provide a brief historical perspective on the development of Hong Kong's minibus industry. In Section 3 we examine the behavior of red and green minibus drivers under the respective conditions imposed by industry structure and derive testable implications. The implications of competition are confronted with empirical evidence in Section 4. Conclusions, policy implications, and suggestions for future research are discussed in Section 5.

2. INSTITUTIONAL, OPERATIONAL, AND HISTORICAL DETAILS

With the exception of the railway corporations, all public transport companies in Hong Kong are privately owned and operated. However, public transit operators, like companies in many other sectors of Hong Kong's economy, are subject to a high degree of government regulation.In the case of public transit, this regulation has as its primary stated goal the coordination of private transit operations to make the most efficient use of Hong Kong's severely limited roadways (Hong Kong Government, 1992). Government policy has also been oriented towards encouraging the use of public transit by taxing the ownership and usage of private vehicles (Hau, 1996; Rusco & Walls, 1998).

The road network in Hong Kong is one of the most highly utilized in the world, with its 1,559 kilometers of trafficable roads supporting 25.6 million vehicle-kilometers per day (Transport Department, 1993). The roadway is even more highly utilized when accounting for the fact that the majority of passenger journeys in Hong Kong are made on some form of public transport. Franchised bus operations are cumulatively responsible for about 34% of passenger journeys and taxis are responsible for about 13% of passenger journeys (Transport Department, 1992b). About 17% of all passenger journeys in Hong Kong are made on two similar types of minibuses (Transport Department, 1992b). Minibuses account for a substantial proportion of total public transit passenger journeys made by motor vehicles.

The Hong Kong minibus industry originated in the 1960s in the context of an underdeveloped surface transportation network.[4] So-called dual-purpose vans that were permitted to carry goods but not passengers were first licensed in 1961. The goods-only restrictions were not enforced, leading to the *de facto* establishment of minibus services. Growth of transport demand in excess of expansion by the franchised bus companies supported the growth of illegal minibus operations. Strikes by workers of the franchised bus companies in 1966 and 1967 made the legal restrictions on minibuses virtually unenforceable, and this further contributed to the development of a dense minibus route network. It has been estimated that by 1968 over 4,000 minibuses were carrying over 500,000 passengers per day, and this amounted to about 25% of the passenger volume of franchised bus services (Meakin, 1993, p. 171). Having become a "used and useful" part of the public transport system, legislation was passed in 1969 licensing the minibuses as public light buses (PLBs) with a maximum of 14 seats.[5] Since 1976 the number of PLBs has remained at the government-imposed ceiling of 4,350.

After the legalization of the minibus industry, PLBs were permitted to set their own fares and routes. The route network evolved in response to changes in demand patterns. The government noted that PLBs were concentrated in the urban corridors causing traffic congestion as passengers were picked up and set down without warning. PLBs have since been prohibited from a number of urban areas, busy corridors, and housing estates. PLBs continue to compete against other transport providers in the corridors where regulations do not prohibit their operation.

An outgrowth of the policy to control PLBs was the creation of distinct types of PBs: red minibuses (RMBs) and green minibuses (GMBs). The distinction between the two types of minibuses can best be understood as follows. The license to own and operate a public light bus is by default granted under the terms of minimal government regulation associated with RMBs. However, individuals may apply for a GMB license which restricts the route, timetable, vehicle deployment, stopping points, termini locations, and fares of their operations. In exchange for the restrictions, GMB routes receive some protection from RMBs, and the routes often serve areas where ample feeder traffic demands higher-quality high-frequency services than RMBs or franchised buses provide.

If there is sufficient interest in a particular route, either from potential GMB operators or government regulators, routes are packaged and auctioned, often with an element of cross-subsidy in the packaging. Having secured a route, a GMB operator must purchase the required number of minibuses. Since the government has fixed the total number of minibuses to 4,350, the purchase of new GMBs necessarily displaces an identical number of RMBs (as is shown in Table 1). These purchases are made in the market. To physically convert an RMB to a GMB is simply a matter of painting it and giving it a number corresponding to its route.[6]

GMB companies employ drivers on a salary basis while RMBs are leased to drivers by the shift, similar to the way taxis operate in many cities.[7] The GMB driver salary consists of a basic salary and a bonus component for being polite and courteous to passengers.[8] The drivers of RMBs are claimants to the residual between gross revenues and costs that include vehicle rental, fuel, foregone wages, driver license fees, fines for traffic violations, and costs of accidents. The fare charged by a RMB varies depending on the level of demand, a passenger's origin and destination, and the weather.[9] The salary of a typical RMB driver is about double the salary of a typical GMB driver.[10]

RMBs are not entirely unconstrained in their routing choices between the origin and destination termini. There are many traffic regulations prohibiting RMBs and private automobiles from turning a certain direction or driving on a particular road, although these restrictions are sometimes binding only during

Table 1. Minibus Accidents, Kilometers Traveled, and Passenger Journeys.

	Licensed Fleet		Accidents		Vehicle Kilometers		Passenger Journeys	
Year	RMB	GMB	RMB	GMB	RMB	GMB	RMB	GMB
1984	3,395	937	990	111	624367	205640	363566	138349
1985	3,294	1,050	966	130	588814	223377	369742	170418
1986	3,206	1,142	945	239	559875	249769	362906	189511
1987	3,118	1,222	920	303	530845	261326	356616	212802
1988	3,052	1,289	841	344	509180	277648	351259	228408
1989	3,045	1,295	738	340	499557	258375	394584	241978
1990	2,976	1,360	747	278	477199	288034	387232	249003
1991	2,872	1,464	653	319	443067	351856	378746	250634
1992	2,868	1,468	664	322	442841	338654	371905	259888
1993	2,843	1,484	566	312	435063	337206	367311	266753
1994	2,672	1,659	567	363	378138	408782	358174	290524
1995	2,456	1,872	464	349	309318	514319	328141	308644
1996	2,364	1,949	571	456	280111	522835	314722	332592
1997	2,228	2,107	360	279	237082	587392	294003	354092

the morning and afternoon rush hours. The nature of the road system in Hong Kong is such that, even when RMBs are prohibited from certain areas, they cannot be effectively excluded from driving the same routes as GMBs.[11] While GMBs are more highly regulated by the government than RMBs, RMBs have become regulated in important ways by the intervention of triad societies at the termini.[12] The triads determine the number of RMBs at busy termini and impose queuing discipline. For this service, they charge two flat fees to the bus drivers: The first fee is for "parking" rights at the termini.[13] This is essentially a fee for entry to the route. The second fee is for "cleaning" the bus and it amounts to a monthly rental charge.[14] In practice, triads only control access to key terminals where passenger traffic is high. Outside of these terminals, RMB drivers are free to operate anywhere and compete however they see fit, subject to constraints imposed by traffic laws and enforcement efforts. As a result of government and triad intervention, GMBs and RMBs tend to have distinct termini (although frequently very close together) and compete along the route for additional passengers.

From the discussion above it is clear that the evolution of the minibus industry in Hong Kong has led to two different firm structures offering differentiated transportation services. The triad society that controls a specific route acts like a monopolist seller of the rights to terminal access. By adjusting the appropriate entrance fee and monthly rent ("parking" and "cleaning" fees) triads can restrict the number of RMBs operating at a terminal. Having paid the entrance and monthly fees, RMB drivers act independently of one another and can be thought of as individual minibus-sized firms, competing among themselves for passengers at their shared termini and competing more broadly with GMBs along their route. A GMB firm, on the other hand, acts like a regulated monopolist with the mandated right to sell transportation services at their termini but with both fare and level of service regulation. A typical GMB firm is comprised of a fleet of minibuses operated by salaried drivers. Because the two types of firm have distinct termini but compete along their routes, the nature of their competition varies between peak and off-peak periods in accordance with the nature of demand for transportation services. The precise nature of competition between RMBs and GMBs and the implications for driver behavior are explored in the following section.

3. COMPETITION IN THE MINIBUS MARKET

To determine the implications of competition between RMBs and GMBs, we focus on a hypothesized route served by both types of minibus and we will distinguish between peak and off-peak periods. RMBs and GMBs are assumed to have distinct (but close in proximity) termini and travel the same route.

3.1 Peak-Period Competition

Demand for transportation services varies between peak and off-peak periods, which we characterize as follows: During the peak period, passenger traffic is almost entirely unidirectional-in the morning from housing estates to the downtown business district and in the evening in the opposite direction. During this period there are few intermediate distance riders so that buses tend to fill up at one terminus and empty at the other with no stops along the route. In contrast, during the off-peak period, passenger traffic is bi-directional and there are many intermediate length trips. In addition, passenger traffic is generally much heavier in the peak period than in the off-peak period. We will examine the nature of competition under these assumptions in each period.

The role of the triad regulators is crucial in determining driver behavior during the peak period in three important dimensions: First, triad agents control access to the terminal where the bulk of passenger demand is located. Secondly, they enforce a rule that RMBs leave the terminal fully loaded during peak periods in the direction of commuter traffic. Finally, triads enforce queuing protocol. By controlling entrance to routes and enforcing queuing protocol, triads restrict the number of minibuses that serve the passenger and enable RMB drivers to avoid destructive competition in the forms of disputes over position in the queue and competing for customers by lowering fares. By enforcing queuing protocol and the rule that RMBs leave the terminal fully loaded, triads remove the incentives that would otherwise lead to destructive price competition.[15] By controlling the number of minibuses with access to the terminal, they can affect the equilibrium fare. The situation described above gives RMB drivers clear incentives to drive fast in order to return to the terminal for more passengers sooner.

The difference between RMBs and GMBs is driven by differing driver incentives. RMB drivers are residual claimants to fares and as such have a clear incentive to drive fast when fully loaded in order to drop off their passengers and return to the initial terminus for another load. Christopher D. Hall (1996, p. 61) makes this point starkly, "Once a red bus is full the driver has little incentive to drive cautiously since collecting extra fares is impossible until some people exit, and a wild ride might even encourage some passengers to flee." GMB drivers are paid a salary and are following a non-binding schedule during peak periods. Hence, they have no incentive to drive especially fast; in fact, they are penalized for deviating from the schedule and are entitled to a bonus payment if they are found to be courteous to their customers. The difference between GMB driver incentives and RMB driver incentives is illustrated by examining a representative RMB driver's optimization problem below.

Consider the case of a price-taking RMB driver. Assuming risk neutrality, the driver will choose the speed of driving to maximize profits as set out in the optimization problem below:

$$\max f\, R(f, s) - C(s) \tag{1}$$

where f is the fare, s is the speed the driver chooses, R is the number of riders the driver can carry during the entire peak period, and C is the cost associated with driving speed, inclusive of operational expenses, foregone wages, and the expected incidence and costs of accidents and traffic violations. We assume that $\partial R/\partial s > 0$, $\partial C/\partial s > 0$, $\partial^2 C/\partial s^2 > 0$, and that second-order conditions are satisfied. The RMB driver chooses the optimal speed such that the marginal condition below is satisfied:

$$f\,\frac{\partial R(f, s)}{\partial s} - \frac{\partial C}{\partial s} = 0 \tag{2}$$

It is easily shown that $\partial s/\partial f > 0$. Moreover, any parametric change which shifts the rider function up, will cause an increase in the driving speed chosen by the RMB driver. At this point, placing more restrictive assumptions on the model will enable us to make more specific predictions about driver behavior during the peak periods.

To simplify the analysis we assume that during the peak period passenger traffic moves entirely in one direction, that all passengers travel from beginning terminal to ending terminal, and that loading and unloading take place instantaneously. Buses are filled to capacity at the starting terminal with no waiting time.[16] Finally, we assume that buses are fully utilized during the entire peak period.[17] In this case, the function $R(s, f)$ takes on a determinate form.

$$R = \frac{sTP}{\delta} \tag{3}$$

where s is speed in miles per hour, T is the length in hours of the peak period, P is the number of passengers carried on each trip, and δ is the distance in miles of a single round-trip. In words, sT/δ is the number of trips and P is the number of riders per trip.

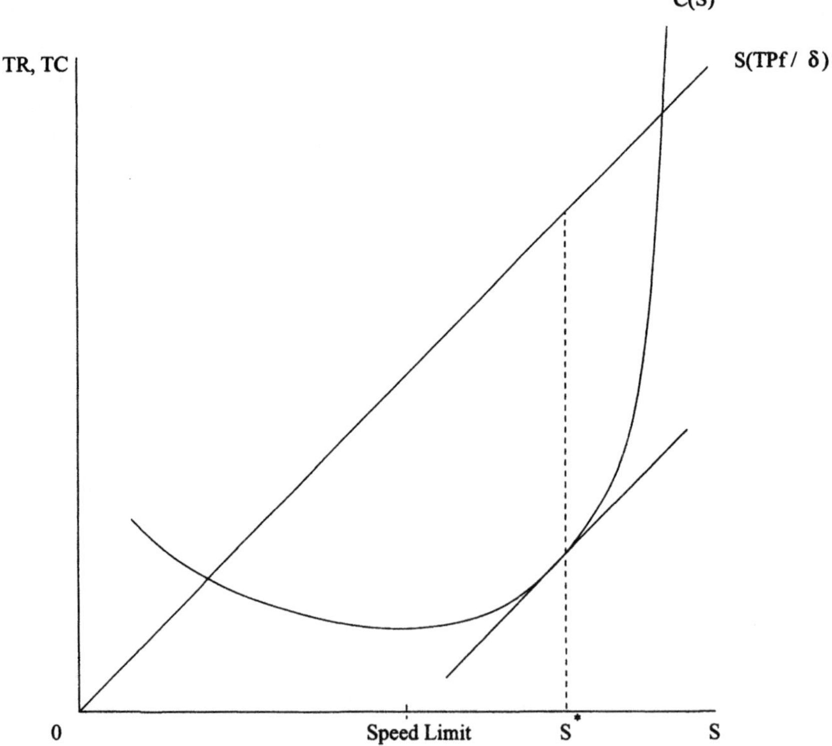

Fig 1. Determination of Optimum Speed During Peak Period.

A representative RMB driver's optimization problem is now:

$$\max \frac{fsTP}{\delta} - c(s) \tag{4}$$

by choice of speed s. The optimal choice of speed is depicted in Fig. 1. It is not difficult to show that the following comparative statics emerge:

$$\frac{\partial s}{\partial f} > 0, \quad \frac{\partial s}{\partial T} > 0, \quad \frac{\partial s}{\partial P} > 0, \text{ and } \frac{\partial s}{\partial \delta} < 0. \tag{5}$$

Some interpretation of these comparative statics will be instructive. A change in T can be interpreted as a change in total demand for minibus services or for RMB services. Such demand changes could also result in changes in f and P.[18]

Given this interpretation of the RMB drivers' problem, we can add some information about the operating costs of minibus drivers to make some more specific predictions about differences in RMB and GMB driver behavior. Specifically, we assume that the probability-weighted costs of an accident are convex in the difference between speed traveled and speed limit, and reach a minimum in the neighborhood of the speed limit. Under these circumstances, we can depict the RMB drivers optimal choice of speed in Fig. 1. Note that around the speed limit, the cost function is fairly flat and increases at an increasing rate as the difference between speed and the speed limit rises. The slope of the revenue function in dollars is (fTP/δ) and the speed limit is below the profit maximizing speed for RMB drivers.

Although RMBs may be expected to have a higher incidence of traffic violations or accidents, this may be mitigated somewhat by sorting among minibus drivers. It is reasonable to assume that driving skill is not equally distributed among potential minibus drivers but rather follows some distribution from poor to excellent. The costs of speeding will clearly be lower, the higher the driver's draw from the skill distribution, and hence, the higher his net income from driving an RMB. If there is competition for RMB driver spots, greater driving skill provides an advantage.[19] Driver income is clearly higher for RMB drivers than for GMB drivers so we expect drivers to sort according to their skill level, with the higher skilled drivers concentrated in the RMB pool.[20]

Now consider the optimization problem of the GMB driver who is paid a salary and is required to keep a fixed schedule designed to satisfy the frequency of service regulations. Incentive compatibility rules out fixed wage contracts which stipulate that GMB drivers take significant risks with respect to traffic violations and accidents. It is also inconsistent with rational government regulation to set service frequency and numbers of buses, which can only be achieved by excessive speeding and violating other traffic laws. Finally, even if GMB drivers can be compelled by threat of job loss to speed regularly, they have no marginal incentive to comply so they will not respond differentially to rider preferences and demand conditions. In other words, GMB drivers do not benefit from driving at higher speeds and so they will not be willing to accept the increased probability of incurring traffic violations or becoming involved in traffic accidents. In fact, as was discussed in Section 2, GMB companies actually discourage traffic violations above and beyond making drivers bear the fines through the incentive component of their salary. More formally, the GMB driver's salary reaches a maximum in the neighborhood of the speed limit and the cost of his choice of driving speed reaches a minimum in the same neighborhood.

Our analysis thus far leads to two testable implications:

(1) *The accident rate will be higher for RMBs than for GMBs during the peak period*

(2) *RMB travel time will be less than GMB travel time for a given origin-destination pair during the peak period*

3.2 Off-Peak Period Competition

We turn now to the off-peak period. In the off-peak period, GMB drivers follow a binding schedule and are generally not full at the point of leaving the terminal. There is also passenger traffic in both directions and waiting time becomes a significant factor. There is no marginal incentive for GMB drivers to change their speed relative to the peak period, but the total travel time between terminals is expected to be greater because they stop to pick up and let off passengers along the way rather than driving fully loaded between terminals as is the case in the peak period.[21] Hence, speed does not change, total travel time is greater and total passengers per trip lower for GMBs in off-peak periods than in peak periods.

Similarly, RMB drivers do not generally leave either terminal fully loaded during the off-peak period.[22] Moreover, the value of an individual fare is lower during the off-peak period, first because fares overall are lower, and second because riders take shorter rides on average, and so pay partial fares. As a result, the value of the rights to park at the termini is lower relative to just cruising the route for fares. RMBs are not required to follow a set schedule and can in some intermediate areas, park and wait for passengers. They can also bargain with potential riders over fares[23] and/or routes.[24] The many dimensions of competition between RMB drivers in the off-peak period is largely unregulated by the triads. The order imposed by the triads in the peak period breaks down during the off-peak because the locations where passengers are picked up and let off are spread out over the city making supervision too costly. While the terminals at housing estates and the commercial hub are proportionally busier, passengers can be found all along the route and frequently take partial trips. This degree of complexity makes a full-blown model of minibus competition intractable during the off-peak period. Nonetheless, it is clear that while RMB drivers still have the incentive to drive faster between stops, they will also find it desirable at times to stop and wait for passengers, thereby imposing travel costs on passengers already on the bus.

The off-peak period analysis leads to the following implications:

(1) *The accident rate will be higher for RMBs than for GMBs during the off-peak period.*

(2) *RMB travel time will be indeterminate compared to GMB travel time for a given origin-destination pair during the off-peak period*

The combined implications for the two travel periods are that RMB drivers will drive faster between stops and should therefore have more accidents than GMB drivers and that during the peak period, total travel time for RMB travel will be shorter than for GMB travel over the same route. These implications are confronted with accident and travel time data in the next section.

3.3 Efficient Sorting and Peak Switching

Given the fact that minibus capacity is fully utilized during the peak period, the higher speed of RMBs implies shorter total travel times than in the slower GMBs.[25] Hence, if the differential accident and traffic stop risk are not too great from the perspective of riders, riders with higher marginal time values will prefer RMB to GMB service during rush hour. To examine this possibility, we distinguish between two types of riders. We assume that riders differ in their marginal values of time spent traveling. This difference can be depicted graphically by a difference in their marginal rates of substitution between travel time and fare. Note that point **A** in Fig. 2. the level of utility achieved by representative riders of low and high marginal rates of time value when they ride a GMB. An RMB traveling the same route does so in less time and can charge a higher fare. Consider an incremental reduction in travel time, denoted by ΔT in Fig. 2. Any fare in the range of **B** to **B'** will be preferred over the GMB fare/travel time pair by high time value riders, while low time value riders will prefer GMB service.

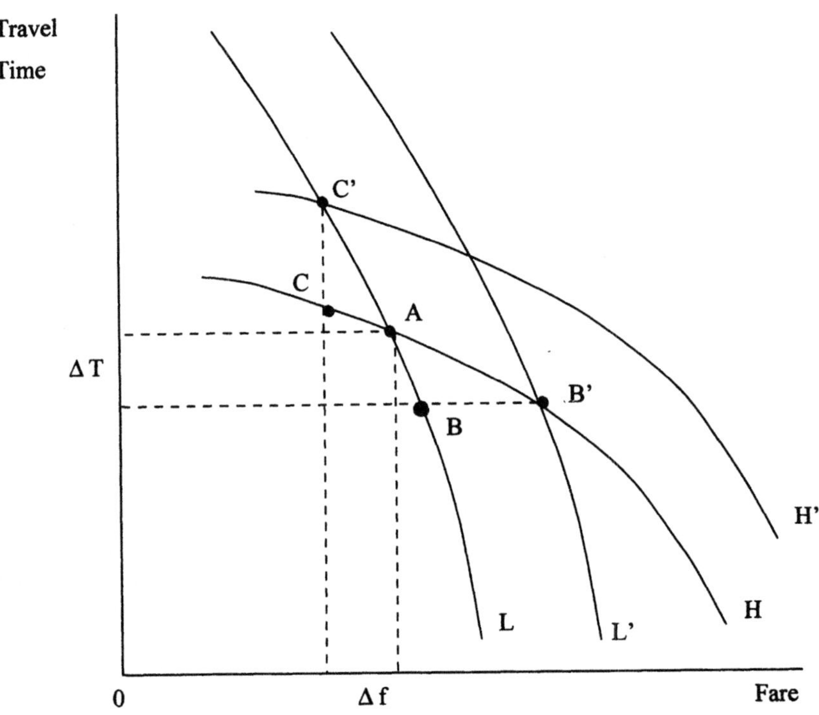

Fig 2. Value of Travel Time Savings and Passenger Sorting.

Now consider the off-peak period, where the primary factor distinguishing the GMBs from RMBs is the waiting decision of the RMB driver. Along a route, there are a finite number of places where a minibus may pull over and wait without obstructing traffic.[26] Two legal places to wait are of course the termini. But because the termini are often chosen to coincide with the busiest passenger areas, a spot at or near the front of the bus queue is quite valuable and drivers can be expected to wait a considerable amount of time to be able to load at these spots. Intermediate stops are proportionally less valuable because they attract lighter passenger traffic. As a result, waiting time at intermediate spots along the route is expected to be shorter than at the terminals. From the perspective of passengers, waiting time increases the total cost of using the minibus service and their willingness to pay falls as expected waiting time increases. This explains in part why one observes RMB drivers haggling over the fare with passengers during slow periods. The passenger knows that the driver cannot credibly commit to short waiting periods and so is unwilling to enter the bus without agreeing on a low fare. In such a situation, unlike in the peak period, passengers with high marginal value of time will prefer GMBs while those with low marginal value of time prefer the RMB and the requisite waiting and haggling. To examine this possibility, we refer to Fig. 2. once again. Point **A** is the fare/travel time combination for GMBs. Suppose that in equilibrium, the fare/travel time combination for RMBs lies between points **C** and **C'**. In this case, there will be sorting, with high travel time value riders opting for GMBs and others opting for RMBs. If in fact this kind of sorting equilibrium exists, then we expect to see high travel time value riders choosing RMBs during peak periods and switching to GMBs during the off-peak.

4. DATA AND EMPIRICAL EVIDENCE

To test the hypothesis that RMBs have more traffic accidents than GMBs, we collected data on minibus vehicle-kilometers traveled, accident involvement, and passenger journeys from the *Traffic Accident Statistics*, *Traffic and Transport Digest*, and *The Annual Traffic Census* published by the Transport Department of the Hong Kong Government. Table 1 shows the data for the sample period 1984–1997. We calculated the rate of involvement in traffic accidents per vehicle-kilometer and per passenger-journey for both RMBs and GMBs. Time-series plots of the traffic accident rates for GMBs and RMBs are shown in Fig. 3. It is clear that the accident rate by either metric is higher for RMBs than for GMBs. The results of a one-sided paired *t*-test indicated that we could reject the hypothesis that accident rates were lower for GMBs than for RMBs in favor of the alternative that the RMB accident rate is greater than the GMB accident rate at the 1% marginal significance level.[27] A one-sided paired *t*-test also led to rejection of the null hypothesis that GMB accidents per passenger-journey were less than or equal to RMB accidents per passenger-journey at the 1% marginal significance level.[28]

Another way to examine the traffic accident data would be to model the number of accidents explicitly. Traffic accidents can be modeled as a count data process with the mean conditioned on the number of vehicle-kilometers driven, the number of passenger journeys, and the type of minibus; specifically, we will create a dummy variable RMB = 1 for RMBs and 0 for GMBs. We modeled the process generating traffic accidents using negative binomial regression analysis and the results are displayed in Table 2.[29] Our results indicate that the rate of accidents is significantly higher for RMBs than for GMBs, with

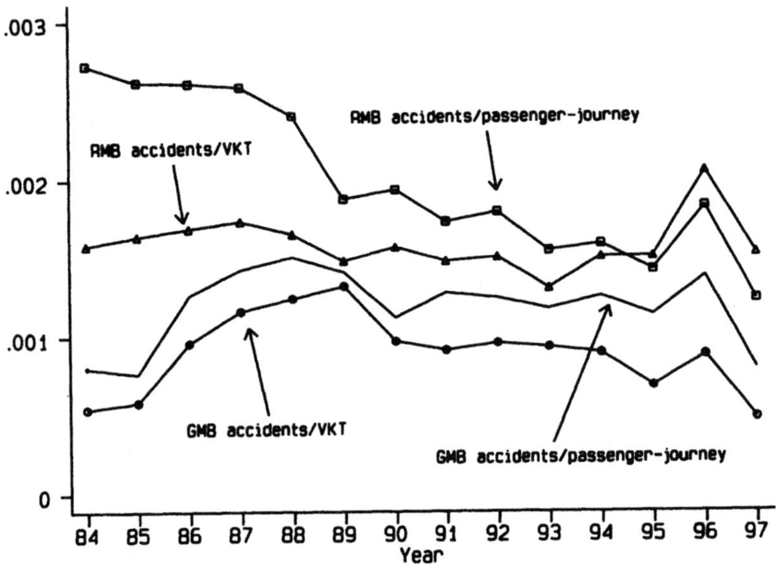

Fig 3. Traffic Accidents per VKT and per Passenger-Journey.

Table 2. Estimates of Negative Binomial Traffic Accident Regression.

Log Likelihood = -166.6853172			Number of obs = 28 Model $chi^2(3)$ = 52.87 Prob > chi^2 = 0.0000 Pseudo R^2 = 0.1369
Variable	Coef.	Std. Err.	z
_ln mean			
Vehicle Kilometers Traveled	1.43e–06	5.99e–07	2.387
Passenger Journeys	2.05e–06	1.62e–06	1.269
RMB Indicator (= 1 if RMB)	0.4974841	0.1468769	3.387
Constant	4.6638	0.2787771	16.729
_ln alpha			
Shape Parameter	–3.195217	0.2888468	–11.062

(LR test against Poisson, chi2(1) = 285.6606).

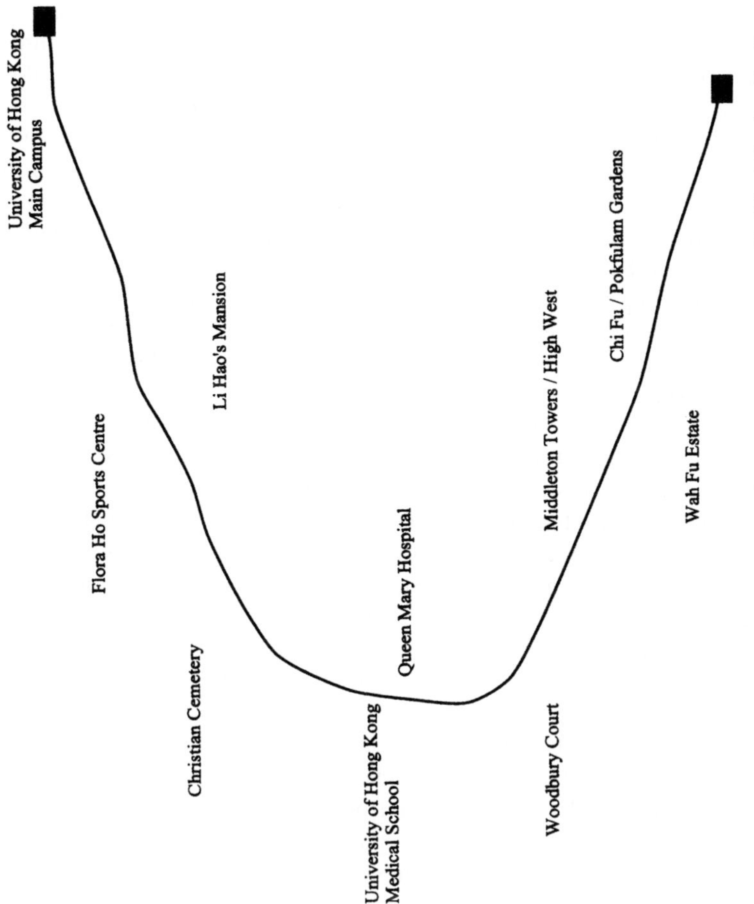

Fig 4. Map of RMB and GMB Routes along Pokfulam Road.

a t-statistic of 3.387 on the RMB indicator variable. The empirical evidence on traffic accidents supports the hypothesis that RMBs have a higher incidence of accidents than do GMBs.

To examine the hypotheses on RMB and GMB travel time during peak and off-peak periods, data on minibus travel times, passenger entrance and exit times, and fares charged were collected. We chose a route where RMBs and GMBs traveled identical routes and collected the data during the morning rush hour and during the late morning and early afternoon off-peak over a three-week period. We chose two minibus routes that have a parallel segment: GMB route 31 and the RMB route that runs from southern Hong Kong island district to the Central bus terminal. The GMB route 31 runs from Tin Wan to Causeway Bay via Pokfulam Road and Bonham road. The RMB route that we studied for comparison starts at Ting Sing Road in Aberdeen and continues to the Central bus terminus via several alternative routes. For the purpose of comparing journey times we focus on the section of the RMB route from Aberdeen to the University of Hong Kong campus and the section of the GMB route that runs from Tin Wan to the University of Hong Kong near the intersection of Pokfulam and Bonham roads. Figure 4 shows a map of the particular RMB and GMB routes under study.

The travel time records are disaggregated by peak and off-peak periods. Peak periods were from 07:30 to 09:30 hours and off-peak periods were 10:00 to 15:00 hours. All figures shown in Table 3 were derived from 30 trips each for GMB and RMB routes during peak and off-peak periods. In our sample of data it is clear that the mean journey time for each type of minibus is lower in the peak period than in the off-peak period: Waiting time and cruising during the off-peak more than offset the lower level of traffic congestion compared to the peak period. In our sample, the average journey time is longer on RMBs than GMBs during the off-peak, but that RMBs are faster than GMBs during the peak.

To test formally the travel-time hypotheses set out in Section 3 we performed unpaired one-sided t-tests for the unmatched samples of peak-period and off-peak journey times under the assumption of unequal variances for GMB and RMB travel times. As is shown in the upper panel of Table 3, we can reject the null hypothesis that RMB travel times are not less than GMB travel times during the peak period at a marginal significance level of less than 1%. During the off-peak, we can reject the null hypothesis that GMB travel times are not less than RMB travel times at a marginal significance level of about 10%.

The driving actor during the off-peak is the waiting time for the RMBs versus the fixed schedule for the GMBs. The RMB queue discipline at the terminals ensures that each bus is full before leaving, and this leads to a headway that

Table 3. Differences in RMB and GMB Peak and Off-Peak Journey Times.

Peak-Period Travel Times

Variable	Obs	Mean	Std. Dev.
RMB Time	30	10.46	1.23
GMB Time	30	14.06	1.86
combined	60	12.26	

Ho: mean(RMB) ≥ mean(GMB)
(assuming unequal variances)
$t = -8.8425$ with 52 d.f. (Welch)
Pr < t ~ = 0.0000.

Off-Peak Travel Times

Variable	Obs	Mean	Std. Dev.
RMB Time	30	18.52	2.75
GMB Time	30	17.69	2.09
combined	60	18.105	

Ho: mean(RMB) ≤ mean(GMB)
(assuming unequal variances)
$t = 1.3162$ with 56 d.f. (Welch)
Pr > t = 0.0967.

is longer than for GMBs during the off-peak. RMB waiting time at the terminal is substantially longer because they do not leave the terminal until full and the arrival rate of passengers is much lower than during the peak period.[30] During the peak, there is sufficient demand that RMBs fill up quickly and RMBs that might cruise for fares during the off-peak choose to pick up passengers at the terminal, resulting in very short waiting times. GMBs also leave as soon as full during the peak, but journeys take longer than an RMB due to the driver's incentives. However, during the off-peak their schedule is binding so that GMBs provide shorter (or at least more predictable) journey times than RMBs.

5. CONCLUSIONS

In this paper we examined minibus competition in Hong Kong between two similar types of minibus firms. The two types of firms are distinguished by their industrial organizations and by the restrictions placed on their operations by government regulators and triad societies: One type of minibus is regulated by the government with respect to fare, level of service, and route, and the drivers are paid a fixed monthly salary. The other type of minibus firm is not subject to government fare, level of service, or route regulations, but they are regulated by triad societies, and their drivers are residual claimants who either own or lease their minibus. The institutional and operational characteristics were used to analyze minibus competition and differing driver behavior under these alternative industrial organizations.

The analysis indicates a potential safety issue with respect to the deregulated part of the minibus market. Specifically, RMB drivers have the incentive to drive faster and with higher variance than their GMB counterparts, and this leads to a higher incidence of traffic accidents for RMBs. However, this must be balanced against the beneficial effects of deregulation; RMB drivers have the incentive during off-peak periods to provide a more varied level of service. They will sometimes find it in their interest to lower prices to attract riders and they are also more flexible than GMBs in responding to demand during the off-peak. This leads to the possibility that high travel time value riders can switch between RMB and GMB service depending on which is the faster and more reliable service at the time. Such diversity of service may improve the overall effectiveness of the public transportation system and enable the mini-bus component of this system to avoid the tendency to cluster together.

This paper also points to the importance of modeling the incentives of bus drivers in deregulated urban transport markets instead of treating bus schedules and frequencies as predetermined. Further research is called for to examine more fully the impact of differentially regulated transport modes and alternative industrial organizations on the level and consistency of transport services. In particular, our preliminary analysis points to the possibility of augmenting the model to include consumers who are heterogeneous in the valuations that they place on travel time. Within such a framework, our ongoing research examines the existence and uniqueness of a peak-switching equilibrium in which travelers are sorted efficiently between the competing types of minibus firms.

NOTES

1. See, for example, the volume edited by Lave (1985) for numerous articles relating to the private provision of public transportation.

2. See the paper by Oldale (1998) for details of competition in local U.K. bus markets. Clustering of buses is a natural phenomenon because scheduled headways typically would result in an unstable equilibrium. According to a public transit supervisor, one reason why transit managers employ "schedule checkers" to monitor bus operators is to prevent this clustering because it is exacerbated by shirking bus drivers who tend to "run hot" so that they do not have to pick up as many passengers.

3. Several previous studies have examined minibuses in urban transport. Walters (1979) argued persuasively the merits of minibuses in a study of their use in Kuala Lumpur. Mohring (1983) simulated minibus operations and determined the conditions under which they are profitable. Bly and Oldfield (1986) modeled competition between minibuses and franchised buses.

4. Much of this material on the development of the minibus industry was drawn from Meakin (1993).

5. There are now 16 seats on minibuses in Hong Kong.Just across the border from Hong Kong, minibuses in Shenzen with the same chassis are configured to seat 24 passengers.

6. RMBs have no number or other distinguishing markings. As such, their drivers are afforded a degree of anonymity with respect to their customers and can also deviate from their regular route.

7. Some RMBs are owner operated for one shift per day and leased to another driver for the other shift.

8. The information on the compensation structure of GMB drivers was provided (in Chinese) by the Hong Kong, Kowloon, and NT. Public & Maxicab Light Bus Merchants' United Association. Ying Ying Wan translated the document into English.

9. For example, one of the authors boarded a RMB when the fare was $7. A few minutes later, the Hong Kong Government officially hoisted the number 8 typhoon signal which permits transport operators to cease operations. The last seat on the bus went for $20.

10. Yau (1995) estimated that GMB drivers earned about HK$8,200 per month and that RMB drivers earned about HK$16,040 per month, net of vehicle rental and operating costs. The rate of exchange is approximately HK$7.8 = US$1.

11. Hong Kong has very few roads connecting major housing estates with the principle commercial districts and transportation hubs. A journey that would appear to be very short "as the crow flies" will often require a circuitous routing due to the nature of the road system in Hong Kong.

12. In Hong Kong organized crime figures are known as triads. It is difficult to find anyone who will speak frankly regarding the extent of triad activities in Hong Kong. According to Frederic Dannen (1997, p. 25), "Today, Hong Kong has more than fifty triad societies, although only twelve to fifteen are active. They specialize in fields such as drug trafficking, money laundering, counterfeiting, and extortion." Our discussion of triad involvement in the minibus industry is based on the first-hand accounts of police inspectors and bus operators.

13. The creation and enforcement of these property rights at the termini would seem to have many of the benefits identified by Klein et al. (1997) in their study of "curb rights."

14. This information was obtained by Yau (1995) from discussions with RMB drivers and Inspectors of the then-Royal Hong Kong Police.

15. Only one bus may load at a time and demand during peak periods is sufficient that other buses waiting in the queue need not lower prices to ensure a full bus.

16. From frequent observation and systematic sampling, the authors can attest to the reasonableness of some of these assumptions. Minibuses during rush hours are almost always full in the direction of traffic and virtually empty in the other direction. The fact that minibus numbers have remained constant since 1976 in the face of growing transportation demand has led to full utilization of minibuses during peak periods.

17. This assumption simplifies the analysis by eliminating a discontinuity at or near the end of the peak-period when the last bus to leave during the peak period may not be fully loaded.

18. An extended note regarding the cost of speed function and rider preferences for speed/safety is warranted. C.D. Hall's entertaining characterization notwithstanding,we assume that the speed during the peak period is never fast enough to cause riders to flee. Riders certainly care about their safety in minibuses, and are surely aware that higher speeds increase the risk and severity of accidents. However, the fact that RMBs are oversubscribed during the peak period indicates that the equilibrium fare/speed combination is acceptable. In as much as the equilibrium speed deters some riders, they will seek alternative means to commute. This could affect the length of time, T, the peak period is in force which will feed back into the choice of speed and theequilibrium fare. However, once an equilibrium speed/fare combination is arrived at, the safety issue will no longer have an impact on the marginal conditions faced by an individual RMB driver.

19. This point is strengthened by the competition for RMB driver positions that involve entry and rental fees, as is the case in Hong Kong.

20. While we have no hard empirical evidence on bus driver skill, it is obvious to passengers that GMB drivers are much older than RMB drivers are. The combination of age and driving style has led to the popular expatriate characterization of RMB drivers as cowboys and GMB drivers as very retiring.

21. The scheduled service typically requires buses to wait at both terminals in order to maintain the mandated schedule, but prohibits them from waiting for passengers at intermediate stops. They are required to stop to pick up and let off passengers upon request at any point along the route with the exception of certain marked areas.

22. The rate of arrival of riders at the termini is still higher than at other pick-up spots along the route. Hence, RMBs achieving places near the front of the queue may still leave fully loaded. However, RMBs arriving at the termini and finding a long queue will find it a better strategy to leave immediately to seek riders along the route.

23. S.N.S. Cheung once related that while he was at The Peak – which is a terminus for minibuses, franchised buses, and the peak tram – waiting for his car and driver to arrive, a red minibus pulled up and the driver tried to get him to board as a passenger. The minibus was nearly empty and they haggled over the fare. Eventually the full fare of \$6 was lowered by the RMB driver to only \$1. About that time the car and driver arrived. Hong Kong makes an excellent economics laboratory.

24. One of the authors recently rode a red minibus in Hong Kong on a Sunday afternoon. Before agreeing to board, the author bargained with the bus driver over the route: there were two possible routes to the bus terminus, one on a limited-access expressway and the other on surface streets. The bus driver agreed to take the expressway if I would board, so I did.

25. The differential in speed alone understates the ability of RMB drivers to reduce total travel time. RMB drivers can change their route to avoid temporary delays along the original route, or simply to take available short-cuts. Their ability to do this depends on unanimous agreement on the part of the riders which they frequently ask for and achieve during rush hour. GMB drivers are constrained to follow the same route even if – as is often the case during rush hour – all riders are going to the end of the route.

26. Note that minibuses are allowed to stop in traffic to pick up and let off passengers except in certain marked areas. However, they risk traffic citations, and perhaps even physical violence, if they pause longer than the time required to load and unload passengers.

27. The value of the t-statistic was 8.728 and the upper 1% point of the t distribution with 13 degrees of freedom is 3.012.

28. The value of the t-statistic was 5.437 and the upper 1% point of the t distribution with 13 degrees of freedom is 3.012.

29. We use a negative binomial regression model because it is very likely that the data are over dispersed relative to a Poisson. Recall that the Poisson is a special case of the negative binomial. In the Poisson there is only one parameter and in the negative binomial there are two parameters. Our results indicate that we can reject the Poisson model.

30. Those RMBs that do not wait at the termini – opting instead, to leave immediately and cruise for fares – often end up waiting for extended periods at intermediate stops. We were unable to collect data on the travel times on these buses, so we do not know how their average travel times compare with the buses starting at the termini.

ACKNOWLEDGMENTS

Earlier versions of this paper were presented at the conferences of the Midwest Economics Association (1999), Eastern Economic Association (2000), and the American Economic Association (2001). We would like to thank Stephen M. Brown, Kelly Busche, Tim Hau, James Keeler, Charles J. Thomas, and an anonymous referee for comments that improved the paper. This research was supported by a grant from the Urban and Environmental Studies Trust Fund, Centre for Urban Planning and Environmental Management, University of Hong Kong. Ying Ying Wan and Virginia Yee provided capable research assistance. The views expressed in this article are not to be attributed to the authors' employers

REFERENCES

Bly, P. H., & Oldfield, R. H. (1986). Competition between minibuses and regular bus service. *Journal of Transport Economics and Policy*, *20*(1), 47–68.

Dannen, F. (1997). Hong Kong Babylon: A reporter looks at the Hollywood of the East. In: F. Dannen & B. Long (Eds), *Hong Kong Babylon* (Ch. 1, pp. 1–56). New York: Miramax Books.

Foster, C., & Golay, J. (1986). Some curious old practices and their relevance to equilibrium in bus competition. *Journal of Transport Economics and Policy*, *20*(2), 191–216.

Hall, C. D. (1996). *The Uncertain Hand: Hong Kong Taxis and Tenders*. Hong Kong: The Chinese University Press.

Hau, T. D. (1996). Income and car ownership: A cross section and time series exploratory analysis. Paper presented at the 71st annual conference of the Western Economic Association International, San Francisco, CA.

Hong Kong Government (1992). Moving into the twenty-first century: The White Paper on transport policy in Hong Kong. Policy report, Transport Branch, Hong Kong: Government Printer.

Hotelling, H. (1929). Stability in competition. *Economic Journal*, *39*, 41–57.

Klein, D. B., Moore, A. T., & Binyam, R. (1997). Curb rights: Eliciting competition and entrepreneurship in urban transit. *Independent Review*, *2*(1), 29–54.

Lave, C. A. (Ed.) (1985). *The Private Challenge to Public Transportation. Pacific Studies in Public Policy Series, San Francisco: Pacific Institute for Public Policy Research.* Cambridge, Mass.: Ballinger.

Meakin, R. T. (1993). Management of taxi and minibus services. In: L. H. Wang & A. G. 0. Yeh (Eds), *Keep a City Moving: Urban Transport Management in Hong Kong* (pp. 169–183). Tokyo: Asian Productivity Organization.

Mohring, H. (1983). Minibuses in urban transportation. *Journal of Urban Economics*, *14*, 293–317.

Oldale, A. (1998). Local bus deregulation and timetable instability. STICERD Discussion Paper EI/21, London School of Economics.

Rusco, F. W., & Walls, W. D. (1995). An economic analysis of vehicle control policy in Hong Kong. *International Journal of Transport Economics*, *22*(2), 199–216.

Transport Department (1992a). Traffic accident statistics. Monthly report, Government Printer, Hong Kong.

Transport Department (1992b). Traffic and transport digest. Monthly report, Government Printer, Hong Kong.

Transport Department (1993). The annual traffic census 1992. Annual report, Government Printer, Hong Kong.

Walls, W. D. (1998). Automobile usage in Hong Kong. *International Journal of Transport Economics*, *25*(1), 61–67.

Walters, A. A. (1979). The benefits of minibuses: The case of Kuala Lumpur. *Journal of Transport Economics and Policy*, *13*(3), 320–334.

Yau, P. C. H. (1995). Minibus pricing under different owner and driver contracts. Master's thesis, University of Hong Kong.

Printed and bound by CPI Group (UK) Ltd, Croydon, CR0 4YY

08/05/2025

01864950-0006